Keep It Simple, Make It Real

Character Development In Grades 6–12

Jan Olsson

Foreword by Philip Fitch Vincent

CORWIN
A SAGE Company

For information:

Corwin
A SAGE Company
2455 Teller Road
Thousand Oaks,
 California 91320
(800) 233-9936
Fax: (800) 417-2466
www.corwinpress.com

SAGE Pvt. Ltd.
B 1/I 1 Mohan Cooperative Industrial Area
Mathura Road, New Delhi 110 044
India

SAGE Ltd.
1 Oliver's Yard
55 City Road
London EC1Y 1SP
United Kingdom

SAGE Asia-Pacific Pte. Ltd.
33 Pekin Street #02-01
Far East Square
Singapore 048763

Printed in the United States of America

Library of Congress Cataloging-in-Publication Data

Olsson, Jan.
Keep it simple, make it real: character development in grades 6–12/Jan Olsson.
   p. cm.
Includes bibliographical references.
ISBN 978-1-4129-6602-3 (cloth: alk. paper)
ISBN 978-1-4129-6603-0 (pbk.: alk. paper)
   1. Moral education—United States. 2. Character—Study and teaching (Middle school)—United States. 3. Character—Study and teaching (Secondary)—United States. I. Title.

LC311.O57 2009
370.11′4—dc22   2009002804

This book is printed on acid-free paper.

09   10   11   12   13   10 9 8 7 6 5 4 3 2 1

Acquisitions Editor:	Jessica Allan
Editorial Assistant:	Joanna Coelho
Production Editor:	Veronica Stapleton
Copy Editor:	Codi Bowman
Typesetter:	C&M Digitals (P) Ltd.
Proofreader:	Dennis W. Webb
Cover Designer:	Dan Irwin
Graphic Designer:	Brian Bello

Table of Contents

Foreword

It can be argued that the refocusing on the importance of character education for school stakeholders began again with the publication of Thomas Lickona's book, *Educating for Character,* in 1991. In this book, Lickona, in a clear insightful manner, made a most persuasive argument that character education has a rightful seat at the educational table. Numerous other books in character education soon followed and continue to the present day. Led by Doctors Marvin Berkowitz and Melinda Bier, there are increasingly well-argued and researched articles that illustrate a strong rationale for comprehensive character education. Based on this interest, there is now a journal (*Research in Character Education*) that is devoted to illuminating the work of researchers in the field. The United States Department of Safe and Drug-Free Schools has provided millions of dollars to states and individual school districts to research the best strategies to impact the social and moral development of students. The Character Education Partnership on a national and international level and organizations, such as Character Plus in the Saint Louis area, continue to assist school districts throughout the United States and the world in their character developing efforts. The Province of Ontario in Canada, under the leadership of Dr. Avis Glaze (2006), released an excellent publication, *Finding Common Ground: Character Development in Ontario Schools, K–12.* This work offers a road map for any school or community desiring to develop a comprehensive character education program involving all stakeholders. Just recently, the State of Maryland has issued a book written by Maryland educators titled *Character Education by Design* (2007) that features strategies for district school and parental support in forging comprehensive character education initiatives. And although the character development of children has always had a place within schools, the efforts over the last two decades clearly illustrate the importance of developing children and adults who are not only smart but are also good.

From this advocate on the importance of good character education, I have noticed that much of the work in the social and moral development of children was receiving its greatest focus at the elementary and middle school levels. Far too often, high schools have assumed that character education has or should have been addressed at the elementary or middle school levels. Once again, Thomas Lickona and his colleague, Matthew Davidson, discuss this issue in their landmark book, *Smart and Good High Schools* (2005). In this most important work, the authors have clearly illustrated the important role that high schools must play in the social and moral development of students under their care. We can only hope that others, influenced by their example, will begin sharpening their pencils and beginning to think deeply about the role that high schools can play in the social and moral development of children. Jan Olsson, the principal of Huntsville High School in Huntsville, Ontario, has been thinking about the role that high schools can play and has offered a wonderful primer, *Keep It Simple, Make It Real: Character Development in Grades 6–12.*

Over the last seven years, Trillium Lakelands School District in Ontario, Canada, has been one of the provincial and national leaders in Canada in the development of a comprehensive character education that includes all school and community stakeholders. This school district, on its own, with solid leadership from the board of trustees and the director (superintendent in the United States), has over the last few years developed and hosted the National Character Education Conference (NCEC) of Canada. The conference is completely full every year with educators from throughout Canada. A leader within the school district is Jan Olsson. Jan, as an assistant principal and later principal at Huntsville High School, played a critical role in working with Trillium Lakelands in developing their comprehensive character education initiative. The model they developed (Figure 1.2) is utilized as the framework for much of this book.

After an introduction to character education, Jan moves (Chapter 2) to recognize the importance of the physical environment in enhancing the welfare of the student. What does the school look like? Is the environment clean? Are the classrooms set up to enhance learning? From firsthand experience in my travels throughout the United States and Canada, I have been in schools that were, to put it honestly, not clean. Now, cleanliness may or may not be next to godliness, but I am sure the lack of cleanliness tells students a great deal of what we as the adults truly feel about them. Going beyond cleanliness, Jan gives examples of what can be done to enhance the physical environment to impact the academic, physiological, and social needs of the student.

Chapter 3 focuses on the importance of adult modeling. This chapter should be read by all educators at the beginning of the school year. If most character is not taught but is caught, then a crucial element of the social and moral development of students must come from the actions of the adults who are ultimately the "parents away from home." Now, this does not mean that school adult stakeholders are always perfect. They clearly are not. How many of us have said something to a child or another adult in the presence of the child that we wish we could retract from the ears and mind of the child? Most likely, we all have done this. The issue is not the one bad day or poorly chosen comment but rather the day-to-day example we present to our students. Yes, one misplaced statement can be hurtful, but we can apologize for this misstatement and proceed to live our lives as a moral compass in the life of the child. The act of moral modeling makes a difference in a classroom and ultimately a school. Imagine a school where every child is being taught and worked with by educators who wish that their actions would be modeled and practiced by all who come in contact with them, to develop a greater good within the classroom and ultimately in the life of every child. This is the important point that Jan wishes to make. We as the adults must become the moral compass in the life of the child. Indeed, this is the reason why we should be educators. Becoming a good educator requires a life devoted to the growth and development of others. This acknowledgment calls us to a higher ethical and social example than required by other occupations. It requires us to model and treat our students with the greatest concern, to treat our students as we would want to be treated, and to enhance their social and moral development.

Chapter 4 addresses the importance of establishing consistent rules and procedures to develop habits of social and moral excellence. Jan acknowledges that rules, although important in establishing an expectation of behavior, are simply inadequate to create a school that is focused on the social and moral development of students. The key is the procedures that are developed to inform individuals of the actions that are needed to develop habits of excellence. He also provides strategies that are designed to build cohesiveness and connectedness for the stakeholders in the building. Jan provides insights into the application of consequences regarding student misbehavior. He approaches this utilizing various strategies including a progressive discipline model that could be considered as a road map for any school.

The previous chapters are informative in developing a physical and social climate where social and moral excellence can be developed. But at this point, we are lacking in developing the intellect of the child. Clearly, we aspire to have students who are developing their minds to seriously reflect and consider the ideals that are so important in the shaping of the moral and ethical person. This is the goal of Chapter 5. Jan is clear in his view that moral and social issues must be developed through the entire curriculum and extracurricular part of the entire school environment. He also presents examples as well as instructional strategies that can be applied to any curriculum or classroom, all of which any teacher would appreciate.

Finally, in Chapter 6, Jan examines the issue of assessing one's character developing efforts. Clearly, a solid research study is far better than a school-developed assessment. However, rarely does one have the money to conduct a comprehensive research study. What one can do is to utilize data collected within the school to give evidence that the character developing efforts of the school are making or failing to make progress. Developing a good assessment plan allows a school to celebrate its successes and determine areas needing additional work. This is important to all stakeholders involved in the efforts. As the old saying goes, "Now that we have lost sight of our goals, we must redouble our efforts." Assessment helps us determine if our goals are being met and helps us work smarter, not harder.

Ultimately, do we view character education as important as the intellectual development of our students? If this seems a rather bold and misleading question, then I ask you to take the test. Assume you have a child, grandchild, niece, nephew, or child of a dear friend that you love. This child makes the A honor roll. Clearly, you would be proud of the child's achievement. Now assume that a week later a friend comes up to you and compliments the child for another accomplishment. This time the focus is on the character of the child. The child is complimented because of his active compassion toward others at the hospital and the food kitchen. Your friend states that this child is always so "respectful toward all people." Now what compliment means the most to you? If you are like most people, it is the second compliment. We all want our children to be smart and competent in their work. But we pray that our efforts and the efforts of others help them become good people. Jan Olsson understands this. He understands that parents are the first role models for children. But he also understands that the adult stakeholders in the school and community also have an important role to play. It is this recognition that informs the true mission of education, to help our children become smart and good.

Dr. Philip Fitch Vincent

Partner, MDed Inc.

Preface

Everything should be made as simple as possible, but not simpler.

—Albert Einstein

I had a rowing coach many years ago who shared with me the secret to rowing the perfect race. She said, "Perfect one stroke, and then just repeat it 250 times before you get to the finish line." Now as a principal I ask myself, "What did her lesson mean, and how does it apply to teaching character development in schools today?"

I learned two important lessons from my coach. First, it's important to *keep it simple*. Designing a simple character development program does not suggest it will be effortless or lacking in high expectations; rather, it must be *focused* on one or two key initiatives that can make a positive change in teacher morale, student behavior, and school climate. Teachers and principals have far too many priorities to become burdened with complex strategies that use up valuable time and energy. To successfully implement character development in schools and classrooms, time and energy will be best used to model perseverance and resiliency. That's the benefit of keeping it simple. A character development program does not need to be complex to be effective in changing attitudes and behaviors.

The second lesson learned was to *make it real*. Where you put your time and energy has to focus directly on the needs of the school, the morale of teachers, and the behavior of students. Those needs can be identified by taking a snapshot of the current situations within the school. That's the place to start focusing your character development efforts.

The main purpose of this book is to provide a comprehensive plan for creating and sustaining a school and classroom character development program. This plan will be based on my 27 years of experiences as a teacher, counselor, coach, and administrator who has paid particular attention to the need for children and youth to not only become academically "smart" but also learn to be civil, respectful, and responsible human beings. In addition to my own experiences, which I share throughout the book, I will also provide information and resources that are based on research and best practices that will guide you and others along the path to an effective and worthwhile character development program.

The book is intended for middle and secondary school principals and teachers, particularly those working in schools where there is resistance to implementing or sustaining character development programs. What makes this book unique from other books on this topic is its focus on the two key elements: keeping it simple and making it real. Existing framework models for character development fail to address the underlying factors that limit students' interest and/or desire to develop positive attitudes and behaviors. Those factors include the students' perceptions about their physical, emotional, and intellectual environments and how those environments are influenced by the relationships that students establish with their principal, teachers, and each other. This book outlines a simple and realistic approach to character development for both the classroom and school that principals and teachers can implement with an immediate impact on the students' attitudes and behaviors.

Chapter 1 offers evidence that links student development of positive attitudes and behaviors to student learning. The synopsis of current perspectives on character development will include a brief overview of successful programs at the middle and secondary school levels. The idea of "keep it simple, make it real" will be introduced by sharing the Huntsville High School journey, followed by the Six Principles of Action that support the framework.

Chapters 2 through 5 outline a four-step approach to teaching character development in the school and classroom. Chapter 2 focuses on *creating a safe and inviting physical environment* in the classroom and common areas of the school. The chapter identifies several aspects of the physical environment and discusses how improvements to them can improve student behavior and achievement. The chapter will be filled with helpful strategies for changing the environment and improving staff morale and student behavior.

Chapter 3 examines the positive influence that adults *modeling good character* can have on students' beliefs, attitudes, behaviors, and learning. The chapter describes the three Es of modeling: Experience, Exchange, and Empowerment, which are fundamental to achieving personal growth and developing relationships of mutual influence.

Chapter 4 focuses on principals and teachers effectively *establishing rules and procedures for civility* without the use of fear, force, or artificial authority. This chapter provides the reader with a successful model based on the implementation of fair and clear consequences for inappropriate behavior, shared decision making, and rewarding and celebrating appropriate behavior.

Chapter 5 suggests ways that curricular and cocurricular instructional programs and activities can be connected to character development by *making curricular connections.* Strategies modeled after *the RITE of passage* will demonstrate how to engage students in the classroom, develop their leadership skills, and help them learn the life skills that lead to a positive lifestyle. The chapter emphasizes creating student voice, community-service learning, and modeling good character through arts, clubs, and athletics.

In Chapter 6, I will discuss ways of *assessing character development* and the impact of a character development program. The chapter will offer a guideline for developing active research questions about how your character development program looks and feels in your classrooms and school.

Each chapter will end with some final thoughts aimed at generating key questions and further discussions between principals and teachers. Inspirational quotes are provided for use in lesson planning, group discussions, and posting on walls or displays around the school. Resources A through F provide useful tools for lesson planning and assessment.

The opportunity I have taken here to put my thoughts and actions into words has helped me clarify the beliefs and values that I hold dear to my heart in the work I do for others as a high school principal. My struggles to nurture a positive school climate based on respect, trust, honesty, and empowerment challenge me each and every day on a very deep level. My hope in writing this book is that it will inspire you—whether you are a principal or teacher—to reflect on your trials and tribulations, struggles, priorities, successes, and rewards in the daily work that you do. My goal, and I hope it will be yours, is to help students learn and practice the universal values and skills of life such as respect, courage, perseverance, tolerance, and kindness.

Acknowledgments

I'd like to begin by thanking one of my former principals, Leo Robinson, who once told me that "the long road *is* the short road." For the longest time, I couldn't figure out exactly which road he was talking about. But now I know. His comment really speaks to the essence of this book.

I've worked for and with 17 administrators, all different. And I've learned something from every one of them. Thanks to Bob Harris, who taught me in my first year of teaching the importance of self-reflection in my teaching practice. Thank you to Penny Obee for encouraging me to go into administration. Thank you to Rick Sellon for teaching me to take care of the little things so that the big things will never materialize. Thank you to Alison Turnbull, who continues to teach me about compassion. Thank you to Steve Binstock for all of the deep talks. Thank you to David Hill for getting me to Tom Lickona's summer institute.

Dr. Edward DeRoche, Director of the Center for Character Development at the University of San Diego, is one of the most knowledgeable, kind, and compassionate educators I have met. Thanks, Ed, for believing I had something to say that might be of value to other educators and for all your hours of reading and advising on the content of this book. Studying at USD was an amazing learning experience.

Special thanks to Professor Ron Germaine from National University, California. Sharing your wisdom has had a great influence on my writing. Thank you for sharing the wonderful reflections from your education students. Their words speak of hope for a more caring approach to teaching youth.

Phil Vincent from the Character Development Group in North Carolina has had a major influence on character development in the Trillium Lakelands District School Board District. He is a good friend and mentor. I never tire of listening to Phil speak. Thanks for the inspiration. Phil encouraged me to do my master's in Character Education and is a valued advisor to our National Character Education Conference, Schools That Shine With Character.

The Trillium Lakelands District School Board is a small rural board in Central Ontario. Character development is one of numerous initiatives that the board and its trustees have undertaken that provides leadership throughout Ontario. Thank you to Director Kathryn Verduyn, The Board of Trustees, and the Senior Administration for your leadership and support for character development. Special thanks to Catherine Shedden.

The Character Education Committee at Huntsville High School deserves a lot of credit for moving character development forward in our school, school board, and throughout the Province of Ontario. I am thankful for the opportunity to work with each one of you. Thank you to Heather Truscott for your commitment to character development at Huntsville High School.

Huntsville High School is a unique place. I think it's a school where staff members genuinely want to do their best and move forward. We could make it a whole lot easier on ourselves if we took another path, but it wouldn't be nearly as interesting a place to learn.

Thank you to my family, Brenna, Rudy, Ali, and Kim. Thank you for understanding that I've always got to be searching for the answers to questions. Basketball kept us together. Thanks Kim for reading the manuscript over and over again. You made it a whole lot better.

Thank you to those educators who took the time to review the manuscript and provide wonderful insights. And finally, thank you to my editor, Jessica Allan, at Corwin. Because of your positive feedback and encouragement, I got to write this book.

About the Author

Jan Olsson has been an elementary and secondary teacher, a high school department head in physical and health education and student services, a vice principal, and for the past two years was chairperson of the Trillium Lakelands District School Board's Character Development Committee. Currently, he is Principal of Huntsville High School and cochair of Schools That Shine With Character, a national character education conference organized by Huntsville High School.

Jan completed his Master of Character Education at the University of San Diego. He is also a professional musician, a basketball coach of 25 years, and enjoys speaking on topics related to character education. Jan is specifically interested in school-based administration and interpersonal relationships and the impact that modeling character development can have on creating a positive school climate. *Keep It Simple, Make It Real: Character Development in Grades 6–12* is his first book. The author can be reached regarding his presentations or other inquiries at 1142 Beaumont Farm Road, Bracebridge, Ontario, Canada P1L1X2; phone (705) 645-1526; email address: keepitsimple makeitreal@gmail.com

This book is dedicated to my mother, Dr. Eva Olsson,
a Holocaust survivor, national best-selling author, public speaker,
and wonderful Bubba to her grandchildren.

Your tireless dedication to nurturing good character
in individuals of all ages provides a wonderful role model
for all of us that follow in your footsteps.

CHAPTER ONE

Living, Learning, and Leading in Harmony

Character Development in Middle and Secondary Schools

Let us present the same face to everyone.

—Lao Tzu, Ancient Chinese Philosopher

INTRODUCTION

There is a shifting perspective among educators about the way that character development programs should be delivered in middle and secondary schools. Discussions with teachers, program consultants, principals, and district leaders throughout the United States and Canada reveal a desire to go deeper in examining the fundamental issues that impact students' attitudes, beliefs, and behaviors.

Highly prescriptive programs, such as those designed to teach a specific character attribute, provide a valuable resource and launching point for teachers and principals looking to start a character education program in their classrooms or schools. My own experiences as a high school principal support the position that specialized programs are a useful starting point; however, they are most effective when applied as part of a more comprehensive approach to character development in schools.

A lot has been learned over the past 15 to 20 years about the importance of teaching good character to students. Working in an environment with adolescents is unique. Teaching and running a school is a difficult task, and the issues are often complex. Gender identity, multiculturalism, the rights of those with disabilities and special needs, poverty, media influence, domestic and community violence, and a general lack of respect for authority create challenges to ensuring that students develop good character as an outcome of their educational experience.

Given the diverse backgrounds and unstable home environments that many middle and high school students come from, is it any wonder why a very large part of students' school experience is focused on establishing their own identity and working through personal issues? And therefore, your efforts to nurture good character must take into account this critical stage of the students' development.

The availability of personal communication devices such as cell phones and iPods, which enable a student to access family, friends, and the Internet at any time or any place, has changed the face of communication. Students are empowered by their control of information and their ability to make decisions regarding how that information will be used. The changing nature of communication, power, and control are both challenges and teaching opportunities.

Understanding the theory about how and why adolescents behave in a certain way is the starting point of our journey. The real challenge in this complex environment is the ability to put the theory into action. The idea "keep it simple, make it real" is about identifying the context where the teaching and learning of good character is taking place and choosing to live, learn, and lead in harmony within the reality of that situation.

Determining who your students are and what you bring to them each day is the first step. Then you need to identify their needs and how you will construct your teaching and your students' learning environments to meet those needs so that positive character traits will be developed. What positive messages do you communicate to students and colleagues? How do you run your school? What needs attention in the common areas of your school, outside the building, around the corner, and down the street?

These questions have been selected to provoke you to think deeply about what's really going on in your building. Answering these questions will provide the context for the deeper discussions that follow this chapter, about what character educators are looking for, and what character education programs will look like in the future.

What is the prevailing trend in character education? How do students' beliefs, attitudes, and behaviors connect with academic achievement? This chapter will outline current trends and then introduce the *Keep It Simple, Make It Real* approach to character development in middle and secondary schools. What principles will you need to guide you toward living, learning, and leading in harmony? Do you have the courage to bring your true authentic self to work by striving to live, learn, and lead in harmony in your specific environment and with those that share your work experiences with you? Let's begin the discussion.

CURRENT PERSPECTIVES ON CHARACTER DEVELOPMENT

Character Development Strategies

If you have already implemented a strategy to teach good character, it's likely that most of your efforts or initiatives will fit into one of the following categories: events, projects, programs, models, or frameworks. A complete examination of the purpose, structure, and effectiveness of the strategies that fit into these categories is the topic for

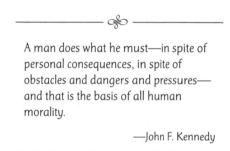

A man does what he must—in spite of personal consequences, in spite of obstacles and dangers and pressures—and that is the basis of all human morality.

—John F. Kennedy

another book. However, a brief overview of each category, along with an example of a strategy, will give the reader a perspective on the wide range of approaches currently being used in character education.

Events

Events create an excellent opportunity to focus on an issue, create awareness, and gather individuals or groups together for a particular cause. They usually have a singular focus. Have you seen the impact that undertaking a musical can have on a high school culture? The degree of schoolwide participation and cooperation between departments and the community can have a very positive influence on the climate of a school and nurture character traits such as responsibility, perseverance, and cooperation among participants. Events that focus on teaching attributes such as respect, responsibility, and citizenship help to raise awareness of issues that touch communities close to home and abroad.

The annual Marathon of Hope for Cancer Research takes place across Canada each September to commemorate Terry Fox and his attempt to run across Canada with an artificial leg. His goal was to raise one million dollars for cancer research. His determination and perseverance, in the face of tremendous adversity, made him a hero and role model to many worldwide. Unfortunately, because of the progression of his disease, Terry was unsuccessful in making it from coast to coast. However, hundreds of thousands of students now participate in the fundraising event each year. The event gives students a chance to contribute to a worthy cause and an opportunity to contribute to solving a serious health issue of society. The event provides a meaningful service learning opportunity and ties back to the curriculum. Teachers can make the curriculum connection by having students write about the character attributes that Terry displayed and relate them to the individuals they are or want to be. Students write stories and poetry and speak about their real-life experiences. The event provides an opportunity for students to examine their own morality and behavior.

Events, if repeated, can also create rituals and build traditions. The annual National Character Education Conference hosted by Huntsville High School is an excellent example of a rich event that has motivated educators and students to get involved in character development. Educators and students from across Canada are given an opportunity to hear inspirational speakers and participate in workshops that highlight best practices in character education.

Projects

You may organize a more complex event aimed at accomplishing a well-defined objective. The project's goal will likely involve a unique venture that relates to a need in your school or community and will require accomplishing a variety of tasks that create a final product.

Whitwell Middle School is famous for its Children's Holocaust Memorial and Paper Clip Project. Whitwell is a small town with a population of 1,600 in Marion County, Tennessee. The principal of the school identified a need to open the eyes of the students to the diversity of the world. The makeup of the 460 students who attend the school is white and Christian. Students collected six million paper clips, one for each Jew that was killed in the Holocaust. An authentic German cattle car, once used to transport Jews in WWII, was brought to Whitwell to house the six million paper clips. The project was so successful that a museum was created. The project has received national attention for its role in raising student awareness of the importance of tolerance for diversity.

The Whitwell Middle School Paper Clip Project lives on through the students. They are responsible for responding to inquiries about the museum, writing letters, and hosting guest speakers. The students also conduct tours and lead learning activities for other groups and individuals. A documentary film was produced to educate others. Graduating students who participate in the Holocaust Study Group are now eligible for a museum scholarship.

Programs

A more comprehensive approach to character education will incorporate the use of a program designed to focus on a specific aspect of character development. Violence prevention, substance abuse, and bullying are three areas that have received tremendous attention in recent years and government support in terms of funding and resources.

Several key characteristics distinguish a program from an event or project. Many programs are developed by independent companies with significant research having been conducted to determine which strategies will be most successful in developing specific character traits, such as respect and responsibility. Each program is designed to meet the needs of students at various grade levels. Staff training, resources, toolkits, and specific lesson plans support a step-by-step implementation plan.

The Olweus Bullying Prevention Program is an internationally recognized program in use by many school districts. The program was developed by Dr. Dan Olweus, a Norwegian researcher whose original work on bullying was published in Sweden in 1973 and then later in the United States in a book entitled *Aggression in the Schools: Bullying and Whipping Boys* (1978). His work was motivated by the 1983 triple suicide of three Norwegian adolescents that resulted from severe bullying.

The two-year program emphasizes creating a committee, surveying the students, establishing rules and procedures for dealing with and reporting bullying, teacher and parent engagement, conducting weekly classroom meetings, and organizing events to teach and promote positive student behavior. Successful implementation of the program requires a commitment to teacher training and adherence to the implementation guideline.

What makes character development programs, like the Olweus Bullying Prevention Program, so successful? First, the plan is built around a school climate assessment. Therefore, each program targets the specific needs of that particular school. Second, the program is year round, unlike a one-time event or special project which comes and then ends. Third, it is a research-based program.

Models and Frameworks

The use of a model or framework provides a comprehensive approach to character education. Unlike programs, models do not provide a single script for schools to follow. Rather, they provide a set of guiding principles or criteria by which a comprehensive character education program can be developed. Once a model is adopted then the selection of purposeful events, projects, and programs can be made to support the implementation of the model. Dr. Philip Fitch Vincent's *Developing Character in Students* (1999) and Dr. Edward DeRoche and Mary William's *Educating Hearts and Minds: A Comprehensive Character Education Framework* (1998) are two excellent books that give examples of models or frameworks with guiding principles for developing a character education program in schools.

The most recent and widely regarded work in developing a set of guiding principles was completed by Thomas Lickona, Eric Schaps, and Catherine Lewis (1994). Their research forms the foundation of the 11 guiding principles established by the Character Education Partnership, a national nonprofit character education organization. The principles outline a holistic approach to the character movement. The approach includes establishing a set of core values that are widely accepted by the school community. It promotes character taught implicitly and explicitly through academics and extracurricular activities with a focus on the climate of the school and building positive relationships. It recognizes that schools are a reflection of society, and therefore, it is important to make the natural connections between the curriculum and issues that concern everyone. Leadership from within the school system and the wider community is the driving force behind sustaining a character education program. Adults are called upon to model good character. Evaluation and reflection are essential.

In Canada, a more recent model has been published by the Ontario Ministry of Education under the leadership of Dr. Avis Glaze, a national leader in character education. Dr. Glaze's *Finding Common Ground: Character Development in Ontario Schools, K–12* (2006) has received wide acclaim for its focus on supporting student achievement through community, culture, and caring. The model emphasizes the importance of recognizing diversity in a democratic society. Teacher, student, and community engagement are at the heart of character development.

ACADEMIC ACHIEVEMENT AND STUDENTS' BELIEFS, ATTITUDES, AND BEHAVIORS

Character Education Assessment

Unfortunately, limited attention has been given to the study of character education programs and the positive effect they have on academic achievement. However, a desire among educators to apply a school- and district-wide assessment that examines the impact of character development is growing.

———————— ⚬ ————————

Don't measure yourself by what you have accomplished, but by what you should have accomplished with your abilities.

—John Wooden, NCAA
Hall of Fame basketball coach

Elementary and Middle School

A 2003 study, *The Relationship of Character Education Implementation and Academic Achievement in Elementary Schools* (Benninga, Berkowitz, Kuehn, & Smith, 2003), examined 681 elementary schools in California. The research compared schools that rated high on a character education program rubric to their SAT9 and California Academic Performance Index scores, a state measure of overall academic performance. The data supported a correlation between schools with strong character education scores and higher academic scores. This finding is significant in that it supports the position that schools that focus on developing positive attributes of good character, such as respect, responsibility, and citizenship, also demonstrate high academic success. Other characteristics of these schools included attention to a clean and safe physical environment, parent and teacher modeling, and a focus on student contribution to community. All of these attributes will be discussed further in later chapters of this book.

Kenneth Leithwood, from the Ontario Institute for Studies in Education; Lucie Leonard, from the National Crime Prevention Center of Canada; and Sandra Dean, a former elementary principal in the Durham Region of Ontario, conducted a study on the academic benefits of *Creating Safe and Caring Communities in Canada: Together We Light the Way,* a framework for character development (Dean, Leithwood, & Leonard, 2004). The framework focused on fostering teamwork, academic achievement, and respect by using a variety of guiding principles, pillars, cultural components, specific programs, and overlaying strategies. The study piloted four schools over three years. The data collected, using the Canadian Test of Basic Skills, showed that students in the program met or exceeded academic grade expectations by the end of the three-year study period. The study concluded that the framework created a behavioral foundation for learning based on a safe and caring learning environment.

Secondary School

Smart and Good High Schools: Integrating Excellence and Ethics for Success in Schools, Work, and Beyond (Lickona & Davidson, 2005) is the most comprehensive study of student success and the integration of character education programs at the high school level. In 2005, Thomas Lickona and Matt Davidson examined 24 high schools from across the United States that had received recognition for programs of excellence. Classroom observation, interviews, and the analysis of specific character development programs were used to capture the qualities of these schools. The study generated a character development framework with six key components: shared purpose and identity, aligned practices with research, having a voice, taking responsibility, practicing collective responsibility, and grappling with tough issues, which all contributed to a school culture focused on excellence and ethics. The Smart and Good High Schools study identified a strong correlation between the presence of the six components and achieving overall excellence in a school.

Positive Behavior Interventions and Supports

Positive Behaviors Intervention and Supports (PBIS) is an example of a specific approach that targets a "wide range of systematic and individualized strategies aimed at improving individual quality of life" (Lassen, Steele, & Sailor, 2006). The program requires the collection of data, making it a leader in the assessment of good behavior. PBIS emphasizes setting up environments for success and then reinforcing positive behavior rather than consequences for negative behavior. Staff training is extensive. Stephen Lassen, Michael Steele, and Wayne Sailor's study of urban middle schools examined the relationship between implementing PBIS and academic achievement. The specific behaviors that the study program targeted included responsibility, respectfulness, readiness to learn, cooperation, being safe, and honesty. Settings outside the classroom such as the hallways, cafeteria, and assembly areas were also observed. The study found that schools that implemented the PBIS model had higher scores on math and reading achievement tests and fewer office referrals and suspensions.

Keep It Simple, Make It Real

The Huntsville High School Story

In the fall of 2000, after 11 years as department head of physical education and student services, I became the vice principal of Huntsville High School. The school is situated in a rural region of Central Ontario that ranks among the lowest in the Province of Ontario for family income and average level of family education. The student population of approximately 1,150 is almost entirely white. The school has 80 teachers who service students with a wide range of socioeconomic backgrounds.

Perhaps it has been the influence of my mother, Dr. Eva Olsson, a Holocaust survivor, Canadian national best-selling author, and public speaker, who has motivated me to seek and to understand the factors that contribute to the development of good character in one's self and others.

I had an opportunity my first year as vice principal to learn about the school's culture and attempt to define my role. My goal was to find a meaningful way to contribute to the school's overall improvement and influence positive staff and student behavior. My nine-year tenure as an administrator at Huntsville High has become a rich and challenging journey of discovery, working hard with the staff at the school and learning from the best in the field of character education.

Simplicity is the ultimate sophistication.

—Leonardo da Vinci

It began in earnest in the spring of 2002 when I had the opportunity to participate in a board-sponsored Covey Leadership workshop. I took three staff members who I thought might be interested in making some changes at the school. During the workshop, we identified several potential goals to improve school climate, teacher morale, and student behavior. We returned to the school enthusiastic about our ideas. However, we didn't follow up with a concrete plan immediately. That same spring I was selected to attend a three-day leadership conference in Toronto called Schools That Learn. It was based on Peter Senge's book *The Fifth Discipline* (1990). One of the keynote speaker's comments regarding typical school cultures—"learn or we will hurt you"—left a deep impression on me. The speaker was Roland Barth. Another speaker, Michele Borba, spoke passionately about the value of using multiple intelligences to personalize each child's education.

That June, the director of our school board took a group of us to Tom Lickona's Summer Institute in Cortland, New York. There, I heard Kevin Ryan, Hal Urban, and Tom Lickona speak. The institute was my first formal introduction to character education. After these conference experiences, I knew that improving our school climate, teacher morale, and student behavior was where I wanted to direct my energy as an administrator. These professional development activities provided a different viewpoint on how to address change in these areas. I realized I had a responsibility to return to Huntsville High School and introduce character education as a possible way to improve school climate, teacher morale, and student behavior.

I conducted a staff survey that examined six correlates of effective schools to find out how teachers felt about the school as a teaching and learning community. The survey compared how important staff viewed each correlate, with how evident they felt that correlate was in the school. Table 1.1 Huntsville High School Climate Survey Responses, shows the results of the survey.

Staff identified two areas of significant concern: a clean, safe, and inviting physical environment and student behavior.

A Character Education Committee was formed from a group of 15 volunteer staff members. The committee reviewed the ideas and material from the three professional development activities, as well as the results of the staff survey. During the first year, the committee's efforts focused on improving the physical environment of the school. Vandalism, graffiti, and a general state of disrepair were specific concerns

Table 1.1   Huntsville High School Climate Survey Responses:
Percentage of Priority Minus Percentage of Perception Equals
Percentage of Need

Categories	Perception How Evident	Priority How Important	Need Differential
Student involvement and responsibility	73%	85%	+12%
Clean, safe, and inviting physical environment	71%	89%	+18%
Student recognition	73%	88%	+15%
Positive student behavior	67%	91%	+24%
Parent involvement and support	76%	84%	+8%
High expectations for all students	77%	90%	+13%

identified by the staff. The common areas, such as the cafeteria, hallways, office spaces, and staff room, required restorative work.

The committee's plan to improve the physical condition of the building was not readily accepted by the teachers. They did not see how the simple approach of enhancing the physical environment could have a positive impact on student behavior. However, as teachers began to see real changes in both the physical building and student behavior, support for character education slowly began to grow. The results of a follow-up survey administered two years later showed that about 86% of staff agreed or strongly agreed that the school was a safe working environment— up from 71% in the original survey. Now 71% agreed or strongly agreed that most classes were orderly and free of disruption—up from 67%.

Establishing a New Context for Character Development

Keep It Simple

Character education may be most effective when it is approached one step at a time. Be selective about your content. Select one thing to work on. Limit your goals to one or two each year. Commit to a plan and stick with it. Then evaluate your progress before moving on to another target. Many benefits will result from mastering one challenge successfully. The organization, cooperation, time management, and communication skills developed from focusing on one simple goal has transferability to the next priority. Once the goal is reached, then you must keep coming back to it over and over again to ensure that your efforts will be sustained. Move ahead slowly and keep things simple.

Make It Real

The Huntsville High School story is about context. We focused our character education efforts on the physical environment because that's what our staff said was important to them. Students did not respect their environment. Vandalism and graffiti were common place. The results of another survey administered to staff, students, and parents in 2007 continued to identify the physical environment as a priority. It's no surprise. As hard as we have worked at making changes to the physical plant, the reality is that the school is over 60 years old, and individuals tend to perceive it in a negative light.

Character development can be achieved in your school or classroom by addressing the real issues. For example, if you are a teacher and rudeness and disrespectful behavior are an issue in your classroom, then creating rules and procedures for civility might be the focus of your character development efforts with your students. Your goal will be to develop respect for self and others in your students. If you are a school principal and there are behavior issues in the common areas of the school, then being visible and modeling good behavior throughout the hallways could be your focus for changing the beliefs, attitudes, and behaviors of staff and students. These strategies do not require expensive resources. However, they do require a fundamental understanding of the concepts described in this book.

———————— ❧ ————————

Principles of Action

Figure 1.1, Principles of Action, illustrates the relationship between the two theoretical concepts, "keep it simple"

A woodpecker can tap 20 times on a thousand trees and get nowhere, but stay busy. Or he can tap 20 thousand times on one tree and get dinner.

—Seth Godin (2007)

———————————————

and "make it real," and six principles that support living, learning, and leading in harmony.

Figure 1.1   Principles of Action

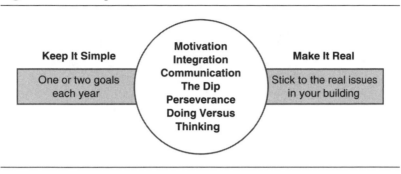

Principle 1: Motivation

You are highly educated. Your skill set is growing each day in response to your experiences in the field of education. However, are you motivated to use your knowledge and skills to live, learn, and lead in harmony with the day-to-day realities of the modern school environment. In the *Disciplined Mind,* Howard Gardner (1999) concludes that the most successful individuals in life, be it in business or education, rely on motivation to a higher degree than aptitude to achieve success. Educating to develop good character in your students goes beyond academia. It requires having desire, a strong belief, and a clear mental picture of what you want your students to learn beyond reading, writing, and mathematics.

Principle 2: Integration

All behavior will repeat itself over and over unless an effort is made to connect an individual's experience with the world in which they must function. If you and your colleagues do not challenge yourselves and your students to look at relationships with others in a different way, then everyone's behavior will remain the same. Mark Nepo, in his book *Facing the Lion, Being the Lion* (2007), suggests that "we do not have the luxury of sitting this one out." You need to join together with your students. If not, you will only become increasingly more disconnected from the reality of working with kids. Nepo goes on to say that "there is rarely a neutral place in between." You are either moving ahead or hiding.

Principle 3: Communication

Communication will be emphasized in each chapter of this book. Your word creates all of the interactions among the stakeholders in your school. What you say can empower or destroy another individual's confidence, sense of well-being, and self-worth. In *The Four Agreements,* Don Miguel Ruiz (1997) discusses the fertile nature of the human mind "where seeds are continually being planted." He reminds us that "the seeds are opinions, ideas, and concepts." When speaking to a student or fellow colleague, choose your words wisely.

Principle 4: The Dip

"Almost everything in life worth doing is controlled by the dip" (Godin, 2007). Most initiatives bring positive results in the beginning and then lose effectiveness as time goes on. Muscular strength training is the classic example where early gains in strength are realized over the first three to six weeks of training. The rest of the improvement in muscular strength will take years.

Students respond positively to changes in their environment over short periods of time. My experience has been that the same three- to six-week cycle applies to positive changes in beliefs, attitudes, and behaviors. Initially, students appear to demonstrate growth in their character. However, without ongoing opportunity to practice good character, and positive reinforcement, students slip backwards into their old patterns of behavior.

Principle 5: Perseverance

A former principal of mine, Leo Robinson, once told me that "the short road is the long road." Character development is a lifelong process. Changes in an individual's beliefs, attitudes, and behaviors are realized over many years of life experiences and reflection. When you make the commitment to teach good character in students you must commit to the process, not the outcome. You may never see the outcome of your efforts during the time that the student is in school. However, you must persevere.

Principle 6: Doing Versus Thinking

Stephen Covey (2004) describes success as a three-step process: knowing, committing, and doing. If you don't reach the third step, the doing part, the first two steps don't matter. In your school environment you spend a great deal of your time encouraging and practicing the art of thinking. However, adolescents don't work that way. They try things first and then learn from their experiences. The simplest way to approach character development is to reduce the amount of thinking time and spend more time committing to doing something, no matter how small of a step it may be. Change only occurs with change.

A CHARACTER DEVELOPMENT FRAMEWORK FOR SCHOOLS

The Components of the Framework

Figure 1.2, Character Development Framework for Schools, illustrates a conceptual framework for schools developed by the Character Development Committee of the Trillium Lakelands District School Board in Ontario.

Figure 1.2   Character Development Framework for Schools

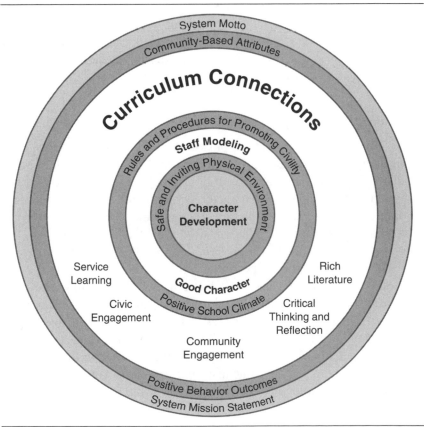

Source: Trillium Lakelands District School Board, Ontario, Canada. Reprinted with permission.

The framework provides a spatial representation of all the layers of character development that a school can implement. If you take a moment to list the activities your district or school have undertaken, you will quickly see that each one may be placed inside one or more of the circles of the framework. Here are some examples of how it is working at Huntsville High School. Our school has used the display of student art work to help create a *safe and inviting physical environment*. Our Take the Five Minute Challenge campaign encouraged s*taff modeling good character* by asking teachers to get to their classrooms five minutes before the students arrive. To establish *rules and procedures for promoting civility*, our code of conduct was revised to reflect the responsible use of technology in the building, particularly cell phones. For *curriculum connections*, our hospitality and tourism students run a soup kitchen for individuals in the community as part of their course curriculum and service learning.

The second most outer ring of the framework is where your attributes identified by your community go. They represent the desired outcomes for each individual's character development. The most outer ring is where your school district's motto goes.

Understanding the Context

Take a closer look at the positioning of each circle. At the core is your target, character development. On the outside are the virtues, the behavioral outcomes resulting from your character education program that focuses on character development. Between the target and the outer circle are the key strategies that promote and nurture character development. Where should you start?

The framework has been structured on the basis of a series of foundations, starting in the center with the most fundamental components that address the most basic needs of the child. You may choose to start your character education program with an event, such as an assembly, that promotes respect. This is a valuable and meaningful activity. However, unless staff model good character by speaking to students in a respectful manner, the message in the assembly will be lost. As part of your history curriculum, you may have the students study tolerance for diversity. Ensuring that the school has a *safe and inviting physical environment,* where students can move about free from bullying, intimidation, and harassment, will also promote tolerance for diversity.

The first three rings of the framework, safe and inviting physical environments, staff modeling good character, and rules and procedures for promoting civility, create a character development threshold. Students can't learn unless they feel safe in their environment, have adult role models they can look up to, and buy into a set of rules that makes their school a safe, civil, and fair place to be. Giving priority to the first three rings will ensure that the school is safe and civil and that everyone values the importance of meaningful relationships.

In Chapters 2 through 5, I will outline an action plan for each of the four inner rings of the model, safe and inviting physical environment, staff modeling, rules and procedures for promoting civility, and curriculum connections. The fifth ring identifies the attributes selected as target virtues by your wider community. Your school or school district may select any number of virtues as a priority. They will be your outcomes resulting from the comprehensive model described in this book.

Some Final Thoughts

You cannot insulate your school and therefore your students from the surrounding community, country, or rest of the world. You will likely be challenged by your students to give yourself some kind of a reality check. At their disposal is uncensored access to information to assist them with dealing with a complexity of issues over which you have limited control. Therein lays the challenge of developing good character in your students.

The character development strategies that you choose to adopt, whether they involve an event, program, project, or model, will need to be simple, sustainable, and relevant to the students' world. And though there isn't a wide body of research to support a focus on character education, you know that success in living, learning, and leading is a reflection of individuals, groups, and organizations working in harmony and demonstrating good character.

QUOTES

While we live in a complex world it doesn't mean we have to lead complicated lives. But often we do just that because we spend too much of our time struggling with life's complexities while ignoring its simplicities.

—Hal Urban (2003),
Life's Greatest Lessons: 20 Things That Matter

What we won't face or express moves into our hands as a compulsion to speak itself through our actions: a sad and empty teacher painting a sad and empty world for his students.

—Mark Nepo (2007),
Facing the Lion, Being the Lion

Harmonize your actions with the way life is.

—Epictetus,
quoted in Sharon Lebell's (1995) *The Art of Living*

CHAPTER TWO

Safe and Inviting Physical Environment

Physical Environments That Change Behavior

To change one's thinking pattern, change the environment.

—Peter Urs Bender (1997)

INTRODUCTION

Much research has been devoted to the following questions: What makes a good learning environment? If the learning environment is a good one, how does it impact on student behavior and achievement?

A student's learning environment can be defined by the qualities of three factors: cognitive, emotional, and physical. The majority of the current educational research focuses on the cognitive factor and how creative curriculum interventions can impact student achievement. The emotional environment, which is formed by the teacher-student relationship, focuses on empowerment and its impact on student motivation, attitudes, beliefs, behaviors, and the resulting achievement. These factors are extremely important and will be reviewed in subsequent chapters. The physical environment includes all of the human and nonhuman elements that make up the physical world where learning takes place. They include such aspects as the visibility of teachers and administrators, temperature, noise, lighting, the availability of space, and the functionality of furniture and equipment. The focus here looks at the physical environment and its impact on the development of good character, in particular, student behavior and achievement.

Studies on the effects of the physical environment on student behavior and learning began during the late 1960s and early 1970s and have spanned over the past 35 years. There has been a lot of recent interest in Europe, in particular Britain, concerning the impact of the physical environment on behavior and learning because of the large number of older, run down, and neglected schools. Nonetheless, the physical environment remains the least studied phenomenon in terms of its impact on student behavior and achievement (Woolner, Hall, Higgins, & McCaughy, 2007).

It is important to acknowledge other variables that have an impact on student behavior and learning, such as socioeconomic standing and parent education. We can't ignore the evidence supporting the characteristics of successful schools, such as community involvement, effective leadership, and a focus on professional development. However, in a 2003 study conducted by the Tennessee Advisory Commission on Intergovernmental Relations, teachers and administrators most frequently ranked a "clean and orderly environment" as the number one characteristic of a successful school. The study concluded that "it is unreasonable to expect positive results from programs that operate in negative physical environments" (Young, Green, & Roderick-Patrick, 2003).

In 1943, Maslow's Hierarchy of Needs clearly identified two factors, physiological and safety, as being foundational to the development of an individual's growth. Maslow stated that physiological needs can control thoughts and behaviors and can cause people to feel sickness, pain, and discomfort. Safety needs satisfy a yearning for predictability, order, justice, security, and a sense of control within the physical environment.

The *Keep It Simple, Make It Real* approach to character development encourages educators to address the most basic needs of students first, those being physiological, health, and then safety. The individual growth and character development of adolescents are dependent on these foundations being met.

This chapter focuses on empirical and anecdotal evidence that supports a *Keep It Simple, Make It Real* approach to creating a *safe and inviting physical environment* and the significant impact it can have on the character development of adolescents. What impact do physical learning environments have on student behavior, motivation, learning, and achievement? Which components make the most difference and why? What strategies can teachers and principals use that will encourage respectful and responsible student behavior toward the environment and others? These are the questions that link to the first ring, safe and inviting physical environment, of the Framework for Character Development in Schools described in Chapter 1. Figure 2.1, Safe and Inviting Physical Environment, highlights the first ring of the model.

Figure 2.1   Safe and Inviting Physical Environment

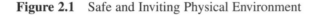

Source: Trillium Lakelands District School Board, Ontario, Canada. Reprinted with permission.

The answers to these and other questions will hopefully convince you that attention to the physical environment lies at the core of improving your students' character and increasing academic achievement.

ASPECTS OF THE PHYSICAL ENVIRONMENT THAT IMPACT ACHIEVEMENT AND CHARACTER DEVELOPMENT

The Case for Controlling the Physical Environment

There is a significant relationship between controlling the physical environment and student achievement and behavior (Earthman, 2002).

——————— ❧ ———————

For children to learn effectively, and for that learning to be meaningful, children need to feel safe, secure, and comfortable in their learning environment.

—British Council for School Environments (quoted from Teacher Support Network Web site, 2007)

Students in poor condition buildings achieve less than students in newer or more functional buildings (*Building Minds, Minding Buildings,* 2006; Earthman, 2002; Earthman, 2004; Welsh Office of Standards in Education, 2007; Woolner, Hall, Higgins, & McCaughey, 2007; Young, Green, & Roderick-Patrick, 2003). In particular, inadequate temperature control, lighting, air quality, and acoustics have detrimental effects on concentration, mood, well-being, attendance, and ultimately, attainment. Concentration, attendance, and attainment are attributes of performance character as defined by Thomas Lickona and Matt Davidson in *Smart and Good High Schools* (2005).

In the Tennessee Advisory Study (Young, Green, & Roderick-Patrick, 2003) students attending newer schools scored between 5% to 17% higher on standardized tests. In the Earthman (2002) review, students attending poor quality buildings ranked 5% to 10% lower after controlling for socioeconomic differences. In some studies, the difference was as high as 17%.

Bowers and Burkett (1989) found that students in modern buildings scored higher on reading, listening, language, and arithmetic tests; there was less need for discipline; higher attendance; better health records; and higher scores for self-confidence.

The Welsh study (2007) concluded that aging school buildings cannot meet modern teaching and learning needs. In addition, pupils' behavior generally improved when they were moved to a new school, resulting in a decrease in suspensions. The 16 secondary schools studied reported an average increase in student grades of 3.9%. Students were reported as being more motivated and enthusiastic about participating in extracurricular activities, having higher standards of behavior, and having greater respect for fellow students.

The Weight Room

For many years, the weight room at Bracebridge and Muskoka Lakes Secondary School in Bracebridge, Ontario, the school where I was head of physical education and health for 10 years, consisted of one multistation, a selector weight stack apparatus, and a free-style flat bench. The equipment was tucked away in a small classroom on another floor away from the gymnasium. Based on my department's concern for student safety and lack of teacher supervision, I convinced my principal to move the weight room to a classroom one floor up and across the hall from the gymnasium. Department budget was used to purchase additional equipment so that a small group of students in each physical education class could go across the hall and exercise.

I created a weight lifting club that was given use of the room at lunch and before and after school. The students were charged a nominal fee to join. The funds collected were used to buy additional equipment and do maintenance and repairs. Student numbers grew quickly to over 50 members. I also encouraged our athletic teams to sign the room out for training sessions. Staff also began taking advantage of the opportunity to work out during lunch and after school alongside the kids. Interest in the new facility was so positive that the department developed two new courses, one for males and the other for females, with a specific focus on personalized training. Our first year was a great success. The growth in our program generated a budget increase that was used to purchase more specialized exercise equipment for the room.

The new challenge became not having adequate space. Once again, I convinced my principal to allow for an expansion into the adjoining classroom, which required knocking out the wall that separated the two rooms. Our weight training club had grown to 100 students. Senior students were chosen to act as student leaders. Their responsibilities included supervising junior students, cleaning, reporting minor equipment failures, and making maintenance repairs. The department timetabled seven classes into the room over two semesters. Local community user groups that wanted access to the facility had to sign a contract and make a financial donation to the program to use the facility during the evenings. The room was not a state-of-the-art facility; however, it did meet the needs of all user groups and motivated them to get involved.

Why Get Involved in Changing the Physical Environment?

The improvements made to the physical environment in the weight room over a three- to four-year period had a number of positive impacts on our school. The room was used responsibly and respectfully. There were no incidences of theft, vandalism, or graffiti over the four-year period of time. Not one of the students had their weight room privileges removed or required disciplining for inappropriate behavior. There was a significant increase in both staff and student participation in physical fitness. Two hundred academic credits were achieved each year by students enrolled in fitness classes. Student engagement was higher than in most other physical education classes. Students attended class regularly and were on task.

The weight room story provides a *Make it Real* context for improving the physical environment where teaching and learning take place. Here are several reasons why you should consider getting involved in creating a safe and inviting physical environment in your classroom or school.

The Physical Environment Can be Controlled

You do not have control or influence over the physical environment that your students come from. However, you do have a significant amount of influence over the way the physical environment is set up in your classroom or your school building. Some aspects of the physical environment will be easier to change then others. For example, changing the placement of desks in your classroom can be easily accomplished without a lot of help from others and will not cost extra money. Other changes, such as improving air quality, may require structural changes to the building and support from your district office. These types of changes may pose more challenging obstacles.

A literature review conducted by British researchers Woolner, Hall, Higgins, and McCaughey (2007) concluded that "environmental perception" does not tend to be part of teacher planning. The reason why is unclear. The decision to change the physical location, design, and functionality of the weight room at Bracebridge and Muskoka Lakes Secondary School was a teacher-driven decision. It required the support of other faculty members and the principal and took several years to fully implement.

When you decide that improving the physical environment is a priority, then there isn't any change that cannot be accomplished provided there is support from the teacher, principal, and if necessary the district.

The Physical Environment Can Affect Student Behavior

A study conducted by the Welsh Office for Standards in Education (2007) examined the effects of students being moved to a new or significantly upgraded school facility. The study identified the following improvements in student behavior:

- Improved during class and around the school
- More sensible movement around the school
- Greater pride in the school
- Higher self-discipline
- Greater respect for other students whatever linguistic and ethnic background
- Increased extracurricular activity
- Fewer suspensions

Each of these changes in student behavior shows the kind of good character that we would all want to see our students demonstrating, all of the time.

Providing students with the opportunity to have input toward the physical changes can be a catalyst for encouraging students to demonstrate good character. Including students in all innovations can build positive relationships, particularly in schools where there are power issues between staff and students (Woolner, Hall, Higgins, & McCaughey, 2007).

**The Physical Environment Can
Improve Academic Achievement**

Recent studies designed to investigate the relationship between certain aspects of the physical learning environment and student achievement have concluded that students in well-maintained and functional buildings perform better academically than those in poor building (Earthman, 2004; Welsh Office of Standards for Education, 2007; Woolner, Hall, Higgins, & McCaughey, 2007; Young, Green, & Roderick-Patrick, 2003). Among these studies, student scores on standardized tests for reading, listening, languages, and arithmetic improved up to 17%.

The Physical Environment
Can Affect the Way Teachers Teach

It can reasonably be argued that teachers' working conditions are students' learning conditions. The Welsh study (2007) identified several improvements in the quality of teaching after moving to a newer school or significantly improving the existing building.

- A high degree of enthusiasm with students
- Good teacher-student relations
- Briskly paced lessons
- Effective questioning
- High expectations
- Differentiated instruction
- Use of a range of approaches to sustain student interest

The Physical Environment Changes
According to the Needs of the Curriculum

Researchers Woolner, Hall, Higgins, & McCaughey (2007) noted that there has not been a significant change in the physical design of school buildings over the past 100 years. The high cost of building new schools prohibits the use of more modern and innovative structural designs, though some school districts are beginning to invest in specialized schools, such as "green" schools. Classrooms are still designed to be square and marginally adequate in terms of space. Student desks haven't changed despite the availability of ergonomically improved technology.

The introduction of computers, interactive whiteboards, Internet, media arts, and other various technologies requires different furniture and spatial configurations that change the physical learning environment.

The Poor Physical Environment
Has the Greatest Potential

It is encouraging to know that the most basic improvements can have a significant impact on the quality of physical learning environment. The Earthman study (2004) and other studies concluded that the greatest improvement in student learning and behavior was evident when poor quality environments were upgraded to adequate standards. Improvements in learning and behavior were not as significant in buildings that received improvements beyond adequate. The evidence suggests that school districts must prioritize capital and facility renewal funding to replace or renovate schools that are below standard. Principals can support this initiative by bringing inadequacies in their building to the attention of district supervisors. Classroom teachers can look to inexpensive ways to create a safe and inviting physical environment for students to work.

Kinds of Impact

Figure 2.2 provides a visual summary of the research and five different ways that creating a safe and inviting physical environment can encourage good character and have a positive impact on the quality of teaching and learning experienced in your school.

Figure 2.2   Safe and Inviting Environment and Kinds of Impact

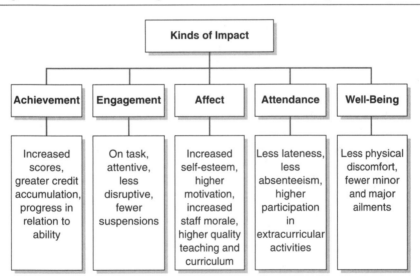

Identifying Aspects of the Physical Environment

It is important to keep an open mind when differentiating between all aspects of a students' learning environment. The relationship between the physical, emotional, and cognitive environmental factors can be complex. The physical aspects of the environment are those aspects that are human and nonhuman that affect the health, safety, and physiological needs of individuals. Figure 2.3 identifies specific aspects of the physical environment as part of the whole learning environment, which includes the cognitive and emotional factors.

Aspects of the physical environment affecting health and safety, physiological needs, and the morale of individuals may be closely connected. For example, poor air quality may result in student illness that may affect attendance. It may also contribute to student lethargy

Figure 2.3   Aspects of Physical Environment in Relation to the Whole Environment

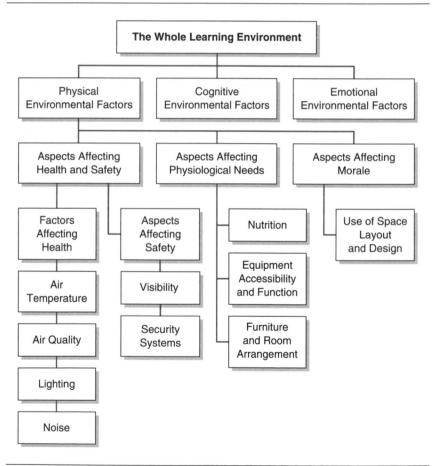

and a lack of motivation to stay on task, which will likely be interpreted by the teacher as a behavioral issue. An elevator used for students with disabilities that is in a poor state of repair, while not providing for the basic physiological need of transportation from class to class, may also pose a safety concern and affect student morale. Let's take a closer look at each aspect of the physical environment. Principals can reflect on situations that are specific to the physical condition of their building. Teachers are encouraged to examine the physical condition of their classroom and its impact on students.

ASPECTS OF THE PHYSICAL ENVIRONMENT AFFECTING HEALTH

Based on an extensive review of research on poor quality buildings, Glen Earthman (2004) ranked those aspects of the physical environment having the greatest impact on student learning. They are temperature, air quality, lighting, and noise. These four aspects, more than all other aspects such as color and space, have also been found to have an impact on teacher morale.

After the socioeconomic status of students, the most influential building condition variable that influenced student achievement was air conditioning.

—Glen Earthman (2002)

Controlling for these aspects of the physical environment may require a broad range of solutions including ones that are quite *simple* and *real* to implement. In some situations, the solution will require a major renovation or the building of a new school. In others, the solution may simply be implemented by the adults in the building.

Air Temperature

Earthman's (2002) review of numerous research studies on the thermal quality of air concluded that increases of temperature in the workplace tend to decrease worker efficiency and increase the risk of work-related accidents. Students learning in non–air-conditioned classrooms scored 3% to 12% lower on subject grades. They accomplished 15% less work in 73°F classrooms with a humidity of 50% compared to 68°F classrooms. Students working in 86°F and a humidity of 80% accomplished 28% less than in 68°F classrooms.

Tips for controlling the impact of air temperature include the following:

- Install proper blinds in each classroom.
- Set the school's heating and cooling systems at 68°F.
- Minimize activity in the classroom on hot and humid days.
- Advise students on appropriate clothing for temperature changes; use layering.
- Turn off computers and printers when not required.

Air Quality

Earthman's (2004) data show a similar decrease in student rank and work accomplished for dust, carpet mold, and carbon dioxide concentration. When classroom temperature was reduced from 74°F to 68°F and outside air supply was increased by 85%, student work rates increased for mathematics and reading (Wargocki, Wyon, Matysiak, & Irgins, 2005). There is an increased incidence of poor health and sickness-related absence in students working in damp and polluted classrooms (U.S. Department of Education, 2004). Myhrvold, Olsen, and Lauridsen (2001) concluded that there are correlations between high carbon dioxide levels, lower scores on standardized tests, and performance on tasks.

Tips for controlling the impact of air quality include the following:

- Clean frequently; dust shelves.
- Eliminate the use of fleece furniture.
- Remove carpet.
- Remove moldy tiles.
- Inspect ventilation systems regularly; change filters.

Lighting

Lighting is the most researched aspect of the physical environmental. Both amount and quality of lighting must be considered for impact. Studies in Earthman's (2004) review supported a 20% increase in math scores and a 26% increase in reading scores over a one-year period in elementary and middle schools where students were exposed to natural lighting. Woolner, Hall, Higgins, and McCaughey's recent 2007 study found some evidence to suggest that lighting can affect student mood and attitude, which might affect performance. Headaches, eyestrain, and fatigue resulting from glare on computer screens were also identified as concerns for students.

Tips for controlling the impact of lighting include the following:

- Install proper blinds in all classrooms.
- Use florescent bulbs with antiglare diffusers.
- Provide task-specific lighting.
- Occasionally take the classroom outdoors to take advantage of sunny days.

Noise

Clear evidence from reviewed studies points to the fact that higher levels of noise, both inside and outside the classroom, can seriously hinder students from achieving their potential (Earthman, 2004). The distraction of noise negatively impacts upon the ability of students to perform well. The noise distraction in classrooms that are at a high level result in low performance, year after year, by students attending those schools studied (Earthman, 2004).

Tips on controlling the impact of noise include the following:

- Keep students out of the halls during regular instructional periods.
- Adopt a 10-minute silent reading time once each day.
- Apply acoustical treatments to ceilings and walls.
- Minimize disruptions during key instructional times.
- Secure tennis balls under each chair or table leg.

ASPECTS OF THE PHYSICAL ENVIRONMENT AFFECTING SAFETY

Before beginning my first year as vice principal, I made a list of my five top priorities as a new administrator. I typed them on a piece of paper and posted them beside my desk. The first priority had the largest font at the top of the page. The other four

Administrators should develop an enhanced hall presence program that ensures that adult supervision is visual during class breaks and during arrival and dismissal.

—The Faulkner Report (2008)

were listed underneath in increasingly smaller font in descending order of priority. Figure 2.4, Priorities as Administrator, illustrates my list of priorities.

Figure 2.4   Priorities as Administrator

Be Visible

Ask Questions

XXXXXXX

XXXXXXX

XXXXXX

The explanation for the Xs is simply that I can't remember what the last three priorities were. I was too busy walking around the building. (I still need to work on my question-asking skills.)

Visibility

Large schools with more than 1,000 students are eight times more likely to report a serious violent crime than small schools with 300 students or less (Klonsky, 2002). One in four secondary schools has a student population of 1,000 or greater. The staff in a risk-conscious school must commit to being visible throughout the day, as it is a key part of a comprehensive plan to anticipate and detect problem areas in and around the school building. Increased staff-student and student-student interaction is also a part of high visibility.

Another very important consideration in terms of being visible is the time of year. I have determined from my experiences that there are cycles of behavior that can be anticipated semester after semester, and year after year, that mimic staff and students. Graph 2.1, Cycles of Student Compliance, illustrates the cycles of behavior over the school year.

Graph 2.1   Cycles of Student Compliance

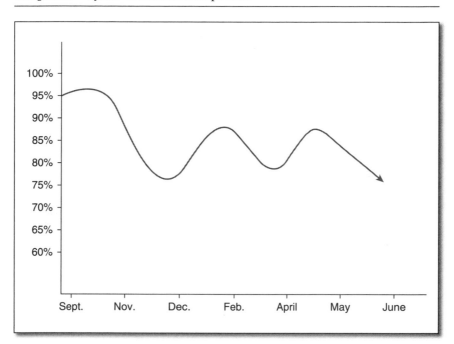

In a semestered high school, the beginning of each semester is generally noneventful in terms of inappropriate behavior and staff unrest. The third week of October marks the point in time when inappropriate behavior will increase and staff morale will decrease; this will continue until approximately the third week of November. This pattern will repeat itself in the second semester around the period of time between late March and the third week of April. Patterns of behavior may begin to surface in a significant way depending on a variety of factors that will be discussed in Chapter 4. The important point to remember is that being visible is an effective, simple, and realistic strategy for changing student behavior around the school building. Identifying and understanding the timing of the cycles, and potential causes of inappropriate behaviors, can greatly assist in the anticipation, detection, and prevention of these behaviors. One of the recommendations from *The Faulkner Report* (2008)

is that administration be visible before and after school, between periods, and during lunch. Here are several other strategies to improve school visibility and student contacts with staff and with other students.

For Administrators

- Spend two hours a day walking.
- Schedule appointments away from the breaks between classes, lunch, before and after school.
- Walk five minutes before each break and occasionally at random times during a period.
- Stop to talk with students, concentrate on the "hot spots" in the building.
- Start from the outside of the building and then move inside.
- Randomly check change rooms and washrooms.

For Teachers

- Adopt a teacher advisor or homeroom program.
- Create an all-school buddy system.
- Take a break and walk with a colleague, at lunch and on prep.
- Stand at your classroom door before the class begins.
- Greet students in the hallway area near your classroom.
- Make visibility in your hallway a department goal.

Security Systems

Security systems can take many different forms. Police officers, security guards, metal detectors, security cameras, keyless entry, and motion sensors have all been used to support a safe and inviting physical environment. Security systems may be considered an extension of the visibility plan. If the visibility plan is effective, the need for these more costly and invasive security measures may be minimized.

As discussed in Chapter 1, the roots of poor character development originate from the real-life circumstances that youth experience, such as an unstable home environment, poverty, and a lack of adult role models. Therefore, electronic surveillance cannot replace the need for adults to be visibly engaged throughout the building. Here are some simple suggestions for creating security systems that are less invasive, less costly, and more engaging.

- Conduct regular fire and code-red drills.
- Use signage to communication expectations for visitors.
- Create a visitor sign-in and guest pass system.
- Do not allow nonstudents or students from other schools to visit friends.
- Issue no-trespass notices to all trespassers.
- Lock all exterior doors, except the main entrance, after school is in progress.
- Ensure adequate lighting in entranceways.
- Maintain contact with the office and key personnel in all areas of the building through the use of professional radios.
- Establish an expectation that staff will report safety concerns.
- Establish a relationship with community police by creating an office space in the school and encouraging police drop-ins and participation in student life on campus.
- Ban the use of cell phones and video recording devices except for instructional purposes.
- Ban the indoor use of hats, hoods, and head gear.

ASPECTS OF THE PHYSICAL ENVIRONMENT AFFECTING PHYSIOLOGICAL NEEDS

There is a connection between the staff's and students' need for health and safety and those needs that are physiological in nature. Aspects of the physical environment, such as the availability of adequate nutrition, well-suited furniture, and properly functioning modern office equipment, may also impact the behavior and performance of staff and students.

Students reporting increased diet quality were significantly less likely to fail the literacy assessment.

—Michelle Florence, Mark Asbridge, Paul Veugelers (2008)

Nutrition

In April 2007, Huntsville High School piloted a breakfast program for students. The program provides healthy food choices such as whole grain breads, fruit juices and fresh fruit, low-fat cheese, peanut butter, and water. The program relies on the support of staff, parents, and community members that volunteer their time to apply for grants, raise donations, purchase supplies, and run the program five mornings a week. Students and staff are welcome to take advantage of the opportunity to eat breakfast at school, no questions asked.

The program was created in response to the large number of identified students who come to school without having eaten breakfast. The program is also used by athletes and club members that are trying to meet the demands of a busy school day. The program has been very successful, now serving up to 100 students a day. At one time, many of these students congregated outside the building waiting for the school day to begin. Now they feel invited to enter and receive support to start the day. An inviting and caring environment has been created for them. There has also been increased opportunity for informal conversation with the adults running the program.

Research studies have focused on the effects of improved nutrition on academic achievement and student behavior. Introducing breakfast programs have resulted in a reduction in absenteeism, tardiness, discipline referrals to the office, and a belief among educators that their students perform better academically in their classrooms (Murphy, Drake, & Weinkeke, 2005).

In addition to implementing a breakfast program, here are some other simple suggestions to provide opportunities for improved student nutrition:

- Partner with the cafeteria service and vending companies to offer alternative low fat and sugar-free choices.
- Allow water in the classroom at all times.
- Provide extra nutrition breaks throughout the day—work with students to dispose of garbage and containers in a manner respectful to the physical environment.

Equipment Accessibility and Function

The condition of the school building not only influences student behavior and achievement but can also influence the work and effectiveness of a teacher (Earthman, 2002). While at school, teachers have a limited amount of time to prepare for lessons, particularly if they are also involved in out-of-class support for students, supervision of cocurricular activities, and the assignment of additional duties. Their preparation may require the use of photocopiers, telephones, faxes, and computers. Teaching strategies often incorporate the use of overhead projectors, document readers, televisions and DVD players, computers with Internet access, whiteboards, and in-focus projectors. Other types of equipment may be needed that are specific to the curriculum such as are used in science or performing arts. Teachers' performance may be impacted by their access to functional equipment.

Principals can support their teaching faculty by ensuring easy access to modern technology. This will help to reduce individual stress and increase the quality of instruction for students. Principals can ensure that the following working conditions are provided to the satisfaction of staff:

- Create a budget plan that allows for the purchase of new audiovisual equipment and computer technology in each classroom.
- Update all electrical requirements in classrooms.
- Ensure that all photocopiers are serviced regularly.
- Respond to equipment breakdowns immediately.
- Provide staff access to telephones, computers, and printers in all department offices.
- Provide long distance telephone access for all staff.
- Discuss with your IT department support for teachers with personal laptops.

Furniture and Room Arrangement

A simple and real consideration in meeting the physiological needs of students involves the selection and placement of classroom furniture. Researchers Woolner, Hall, Higgins, and McCaughey (2007) conducted an extensive review of the literature addressing the impact of furniture styles and room arrangement on student behavior. Woolner's findings support the need for teachers to pay close attention to the furniture needs of students from both a physiological and behavioral perspective.

Adolescence is a time of significant physical growth. Usually, classroom furniture size is standardized, in contrast to the growing needs of students. Students may experience an inability to get in and out of desks. Leg and waist room may be inadequate. Students have reported experiencing back pain that may be due to poor furniture size. Students who have been given access to adjustable furniture have shown significant improvements in on-task behavior (Woolner, Hall, Higgins, & McCaughey, 2007). The same can be concluded for the use of tables over the use of desks.

Of equal consideration is the placement of each desk. Rows are more effective in controlling individual behavior and keeping less successful students on task. Students situated across the front of the class and down the middle isle, within a T formation, are more likely to be attentive and on task. However, student-teacher discussion, in particular student questioning, increases when using a horseshoe formation. Some students may have issues of privacy. For these students, small groupings are preferred. Small groupings provide opportunities for discussion in a less intimidating setting within the classroom.

Here are several suggestions to improve the furniture and room arrangements in your classroom.

- Replace traditional combination desks with table and chairs that can be placed in rows or locked together to form groupings of various sizes.
- Change the classroom arrangement to provide flexibility and complement various teaching strategies and learning styles.
- Provide opportunities for students to move around and stretch.
- Move desks out, or to the sides, and utilize the floor space for appropriate activities.

ASPECTS OF THE PHYSICAL ENVIRONMENT AFFECTING MORALE

The standard of the environment sets the standard for the quality of learning. If the impression given to students is that this room doesn't matter then the impression is that it doesn't matter what they do in this room.

—British School Council for School Environments (quote from Teacher Support Network Web site, 2007)

The introduction to this chapter identified three factors, physical, emotional, and cognitive, as impacting on the quality of the learning environment. Let's return to the question of what makes a good learning environment. Specifically, how are students' learning and behavior, and teacher performance, affected by the way they feel about their physical surroundings?

The Washroom

At one time, Huntsville High School had a serious graffiti problem. The school was heavily tagged inside and out with magic marker or spray paint. Taggings in the washrooms were frequent and extensive. The maintenance staff attempted to remove the graffiti with marginal success by using very expensive sealer paint. With the assistance of a teacher, digital photos of the washroom graffiti were taken, copied, and distributed to staff along with a memo requesting an unobtrusive notebook check of every student in the school.

One day I received a call from a teacher in his classroom indicating that a student had requested to go to the washroom. The student had a red and black magic marker in his hand. The teacher thought that this was unusual and that it may be of interest to my investigation. I went to the classroom and brought the student down to my office. I conducted a search that revealed tags in his notebook that matched the digital photos taken in the washrooms.

The student received four consequences. First, he received a suspension. Second, the student was charged with mischief and had to participate in a youth justice circle, which included all of the affected parties. Third, he had to restore and paint every washroom in the school. Finally, the student had to tour 23 intermediate classrooms with myself and the community police officer to apologize and discuss the impact of his behavior on the school.

Following this incident, I was approached by the Grade 10 visual arts teacher about a project idea that involved using student wall paintings to beautify the washrooms throughout the school. It sounded like an excellent idea. Designs were submitted and funds were raised to support the student work. Since that time several years ago, the washrooms have been repainted by a new group of students. The graffiti has not returned. The introduction of student artwork to the washrooms eliminated the problem.

> If there are displays of student work, then the students are interested in what is in that area, they are less likely to damage the space, and they will defend it in some cases. If they have ownership, they look after it and work hard to keep it.
>
> —A teacher

In April and May 2007, Teacher Support Network and the British Council for School Environments conducted an online survey asking teachers for their opinions on their school's physical environment and the impact it had on teaching, learning, and pupil behavior. The study found that only 12% of those surveyed considered the design of the school building effective for instructional purposes. Let's discuss the findings of the study more specifically as they relate to the use, layout, and design of space.

Use of Space, Layout, and Design

Teachers identified their lack of ability to adjust the physical environment to support curriculum delivery and accommodate different learning styles as a major day-to-day obstacle. A total of 87% of teachers identified classroom layout as the most important factor in providing high quality instruction (Teacher Support Network, 2007). Many teachers reported not having a proper desk and chair for themselves. Students' desks were difficult to move around. Classrooms were too small to accommodate student movement and the proper storage of personal belongings and resources. Ventilation, room temperature, and light were also high on the priority list. Teachers responded with concern regarding classroom environments that were freezing cold in the winter or overheated in the summer.

Space was identified as a very important influence on student behavior. The lack of space in hallways contributed to aggressive behavior. Small washrooms and hidden areas created hot spots for vandalism and other inappropriate behavior to occur more frequently. A lack of common space for student relaxation and play was also cited as an issue contributing to aggressive behavior. It is believed by 87% of teachers surveyed that the display of student work around the school contributed to developing student respect for others and the environment.

Here are some examples of strategies that will improve the use of space, layout, and design:

- Involve staff and students in the design of physical enhancement projects in the classroom and throughout the building.
- Display student work.
- Recognize student achievement by prominently displaying awards, certificates, photos of events, and accomplishment on walls and in display cases.
- Beautify areas of the school with greenery.
- Create soft areas with benches.
- Display inspirational quotes.

SOME FINAL THOUGHTS

Education plays an increasingly important role in students' career pathways, their future health, security, and quality of living. To that end, a significant priority in education has focused on having schools keep pace with an ever expanding curriculum that is designed to meet the needs of the economic world.

Factors that impact on the learning environment, such as child poverty and poor home environments, challenge us as educators to look beyond pure economics and take a more holistic approach to teaching the child. Student beliefs, attitudes, and behaviors are greatly affected by the physical environments that surround them. Placing an emphasis on the development of good character can be, in part, accomplished by improving the physical aspects of the classroom and school building.

Providing a safe and inviting physical environment in which students can learn, discover, and grow and build relationships reaches to the core of many of the most critical adolescent needs requiring attention. Without these needs being satisfied, students are challenged to learn and achieve success so that they may move on from school into the larger community with confidence.

Many of the ideas and solutions presented in this chapter are cost effective, simple, and realistic to implement. However, much like undertaking a new personal diet or fitness regime, implementation will require a high level of commitment and self-discipline on the part of principal and teacher to ensure attention is given to providing a safe and inviting environment. As a principal, you must make it a priority to assist your teachers. As a teacher, you must advocate for your students.

QUOTES

It is unreasonable to expect positive results from programs that have to operate in negative physical environments.

—Tennessee Advisory Commission

Amazingly, we continue to have learning happen, even under these conditions. What better job could we do if we had good lighting, adequate space, good air flow, and constant temperatures? Maybe that should be considered in the No Child Left Behind recommendations.

—Second-grade teacher
in North St. Paul-Maplewood, MN

If this nation is committed to high academic standards, we must stop ignoring the impact that the physical environment plays in students' health and learning. And to allow school staff to perform at their best, we must expect that school buildings meet the highest standards of facility excellence.

—Building Minds, Minding Buildings (2006)

CHAPTER THREE

Modeling Good Character

The Role of Principals and Teachers

We teach who we are.

—Parker Palmer (1998)

INTRODUCTION

Think about the students who come to your school with poor attitudes, low motivation, and limited expectations for personal success. Many of them arrive each day with issues that are affecting their self-esteem, their emotions, and their ability to focus on what you are trying to teach them. These students may have difficulty learning if they do not perceive their physical, emotional, and cognitive environments as positive. Chapter 2 established that a *safe and inviting physical environment* can impact on academic achievement and the character development of students. The physical environment represents many of the outside factors that we can manipulate. Chapter 3 addresses the emotional environment—factors that originate on the inside.

Adolescence is a challenging time in a person's life. One underlying factor that may limit students' interests and desires to develop positive attitudes and behaviors in school is their perception of the emotional environment. Why then it is important for principals and teachers to model good character? You have an opportunity to model the kinds of behaviors that will influence your students' interests and desires. You can have an impact on students' learning by striving to build positive relationships, which will influence their perceptions of the school and classroom environment.

In taking a whole-school approach to modeling good character and its effect on character development, I must focus on the roles of both the teacher and the principal. Research strongly supports the significant impact that the principal has on teacher morale, sense of empowerment, attitudes, and behavior. Conversely, teachers have the responsibility of motivating and developing student interest in learning on a day-to-day basis. In the words of Stephen Covey (2004), it's not enough to know and understand the importance of an action or even to commit to it. The understanding and commitment become meaningful only when we *take* the action. When teachers and administrators model good character, students can see firsthand what it looks like. This chapter will focus on how the modeling of good character by principals and teachers can impact on the development of good character in their students—and how to do it.

Figure 3.1, Staff Modeling Good Character, introduces the third ring of the Character Development Framework for Schools.

Principals and teachers model good character in three ways: by reflecting on their experiences, by empowering others, and by exchanging information with colleagues and students in a positive way. How does personal experience, followed by self-reflection, provide powerful lessons that will inspire you to examine your own behavior in the school and classroom? What communication strategies

Figure 3.1   Staff Modeling Good Character

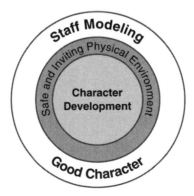

Source: Trillium Lakelands District School Board, Ontario, Canada. Reprinted with permission.

will inspire the meaningful exchange of ideas and form quality relationships with your students and colleagues? What can principals do to nurture empowering relationships with their teachers? Let's explore answers to these and other questions.

MODELING THE THREE ES

During a job interview with one of my teaching staff, the teacher described herself as being "a work in progress"—a statement that spoke to a willingness to work on one's own character. The following three Es describe the work that principals and teachers can do to develop and model good character.

> The real problem with teaching character is that, in order to teach it, the teacher has to have it.
>
> —Kevin Sullivan (2007)

- The First E: The Power of Experience
  Reflecting on your personal experiences can clarify the way you feel about yourself and increase your awareness and understanding of others.
- The Second E: The Power of Exchange
  How you feel about yourself when interacting with others will determine your ability to nurture quality relationships that build mutual influence.
- The Third E: The Power of Empowerment
  A principal's beliefs, attitudes, and behaviors have a major influence on a teacher's sense of empowerment and willingness to become involved in the matters that affect students' beliefs, attitudes, and behaviors.

Making a commitment to the three Es is a challenging task. Daily demands such as running a school, preparing lessons, grading, and coaching, combined with one's personal-life priorities, make it seem like there isn't the time or energy remaining to work at it. However, the effort required each day is very small. Once you begin, you will see that the returns are far greater than the costs. You will become a better teacher or principal and, most important, a better person.

THE FIRST E: THE POWER OF EXPERIENCE

The Power of One

Huntsville High School has a very small cafeteria to service 1,150 students during a single lunch period. Many students go off campus for lunch, so overcrowding in the cafeteria only becomes a problem during the winter months. The rule in the school for many years was that there was no eating or drinking in the halls. Yet I noticed the first few days as vice principal that most staff and students ate and drank in the halls. This was in spite of the fact that signs were clearly posted stating "No Eating or Drinking in the Halls." Garbage was everywhere. The floor was a mess. Food was smeared on the walls, lockers, benches, and on the hand railings in stairwells. The staff complained a lot that somebody needed to do something about it. When I spoke to the custodial staff they made it abundantly clear that they didn't feel it was their responsibility to clean up the mess that others had deliberately made. Students were not willing to take responsibility for breaking the rules and cleaning up the mess they had made. So I asked myself, "Jan, what do you want to do about this situation?"

> There are three things extremely hard: steel, a diamond, and to know one's self.
>
> —Benjamin Franklin

As vice principals, my partner and I both felt very strongly that we had to do something about the lunch problem in our school. At first, we tried using the announcements to encourage students not to eat in the halls. Our personal appeal had little impact. So we started putting students who were caught dropping garbage on the end of a broom or mop and made them clean the hallways. Students were suspended for throwing food or garbage down stairwells. But things didn't get any better.

After several weeks, we decided to do a couple of things differently. First, we convinced our principal to take down the signs forbidding eating or drinking in the halls. We announced to the students that eating would be allowed, but that they should "please use the garbage cans provided." Then at the end of each lunch hour the two of us opened up the custodial slop room and pulled out one wet mop, one broom, and a dust pan. Together, we cleaned each hallway of the school.

The first reaction from everyone was laughter. Then people began to make comments like, "Hey, Mr. Olsson, you're really good at that!" Or they would ask questions like, "Are you getting paid to do that?" I was approached by a staff member who wanted to discuss the ethical value of my actions. There was talk of a grievance being filed against me for doing the work of the custodians. We listened but continued modeling the behavior we expected from others.

Slowly but surely, we began noticing a difference in the halls. However, it took a long time. Over the next three years, I modeled the behavior that I was looking for in the students and the staff. It was in the spring of the fourth year that I realized the lesson of the power of one. I was up on the second floor doing the walk between classes. I had just come up the stairwell when I noticed a teacher walking at the far end of the hallway. As they approached a piece of garbage on the floor, they reached down and picked it up and continued along the way. Later that day, I went to pick up some garbage that was close to where some students were standing. A student said "That's okay Mr. Olsson; don't worry about that—I'll get it for you." That same situation happened on two more occasions that day. Garbage cans were getting filled up. The halls were beginning to look much better. Teachers were starting to comment on the improvements that they were seeing. The custodians began supporting the effort. Modeling was starting to influence the behavior of others.

This story is an interesting example of how difficult it can be to model good character. I have asked myself, "Why did my efforts to model responsibility and caring take so long to bring about a positive change in the attitudes and behaviors of students and teachers?" During those four years, I also had many doubts about how I was being perceived by the faculty. I asked myself several questions. Were teachers angry because they were feeling guilty about their efforts to solve the problem? Did the custodial support staff feel I was doing their job? Was my principal feeling that I should have been spending more time doing my assigned duties? How were the students reacting to my strategy to solve this problem?

The power of this experience helped me to clarify what I valued and why I had chosen to model good character. It also increased my awareness of how others were feeling about the school climate and their attitude toward the leadership in the school. I learned that it takes perseverance and resiliency to bring about change.

The Wall of Vulnerability

Much has been written on the role that self-esteem plays in interpreting our work experiences. Self-esteem relates to an individual's sense of self-worth and can affect behavior and performance (Blascovich & Tomaka, 1991). Whether you are teaching, meeting with a colleague, or engaging in staffroom banter, you cannot help but project to others your feelings about who you are and how you feel about yourself.

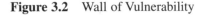

> Vulnerability is a door to new relationships, new opportunities, new ways to grow, and new ways to live and grow together.
>
> —Kent Keith, author

If your feelings are negative, you may feel vulnerable to criticism. To protect yourself from becoming more vulnerable, you may impose a boundary between yourself and others that will limit your ability to be authentic in your day-to-day interactions.

Let's examine how the self-esteem of teachers can affect their behavior with students. The boundary that is imposed by teachers when interacting with their students is described in Figure 3.2, Wall of Vulnerability, which shows a protective barrier between teachers and students when teachers are not feeling confident about their ability to teach.

Figure 3.2   Wall of Vulnerability

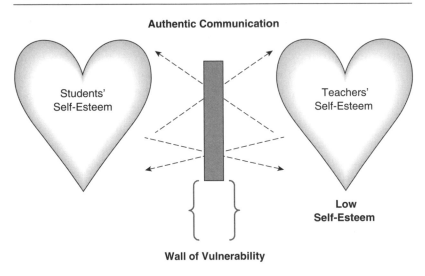

The wall represents an imposed communication boundary created by teachers to protect themselves from being put in a vulnerable position.

How might the teachers' self-esteem affect the nature of the barrier? Figure 3.3, Breaking the Wall of Vulnerability, shows teachers having greater self-esteem. The wall has become permeable, allowing for the teachers to be more authentic when they communicate. The teachers allow themselves to be put in a more vulnerable position, thus instilling the trust in the students required to build positive relationships.

Figure 3.3   Breaking the Wall of Vulnerability

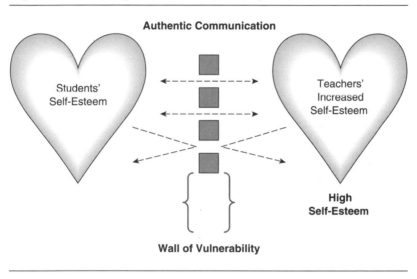

The way you interpret your personal experiences can provide powerful lessons about your own self-esteem, feelings of self-worth, and why you are limiting your interactions with others, particularly your students. For example, a teacher has been assigned a Grade 12 university-level chemistry class, never having taught the class before. The students enrolled in the class are honor roll candidates with high skills, very strong parental support, and high expectations for success. The teacher is feeling insecure about delivering the curriculum, and the students sense the teacher's feelings of insecurity. Figure 3.4, Factors Affecting Vulnerability, lists some of the factors that will affect the way the teacher and students are feeling in this situation.

Figure 3.4   Factors Affecting Vulnerability

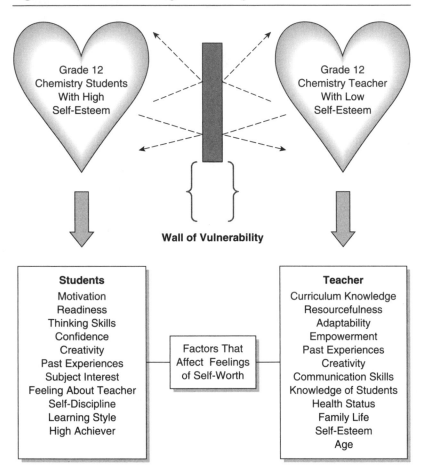

You must examine your comfort level regarding your curriculum knowledge, your teaching skills, age, and so on, and how these may be affecting your interaction with your students and your delivery of the lesson. In terms of modeling good character, the confidence you have in your ability to teach, and your willingness to reflect on your practice, will have a significant impact on the quality of interactions with the students in your classes.

You may choose to impose a boundary to prevent being placed in a position of vulnerability. It may be that you are not aware of this because it has been an established pattern since your first days of teaching. You may have come to the point now where you are directing behaviors, such as anger or frustration, toward your students. The students' feelings about your competencies and their own ability to achieve, be motivated, and self-disciplined may also be affecting their interactions with you.

What strategies can teachers and principals use to work through feelings of vulnerability? The answer requires an examination of your experiences and a commitment to doing inner work every day.

Modeling Inner Work

Inner work enables you to question yourself about what values you currently hold deep inside. Since modeling good character requires trust, respect, and living honestly in front of our students and colleagues, this work is essential. The pages that follow describe the process of self-reflection, what it is, and what exercises you can practice to engage in inner work for personal growth.

> I realize that the expectations I have for my students' behavior and achievement must first be seen in me.
>
> —Christina Avila,
> instructor at San Jose City College

> By three methods we may learn wisdom: first, by reflection, which is noblest; second, by imitation, which is easiest; and third, by experience, which is the most bitter.
>
> —Confucious

Self-Reflection

Learning more about yourself and your fundamental nature as a human being connects you with your values and your students and colleagues and increases your ability to model good character. Figure 3.5, Cycle of Reflection, identifies the process.

Figure 3.5 Cycle of Reflection

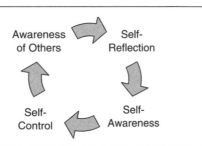

The cycle is based on the work of organizational consultant Lionel Stapley (2006). Communicating openly with students, other teachers, your principal, or, if you are a principal, with your staff, may leave you feeling highly vulnerable. As demonstrated in the case of the Grade 12 chemistry teacher, teachers face this challenge every time they step in front of a group of students or peers. Principals may feel vulnerable when setting expectations for teachers. Taking the time for self-reflection gives you a greater awareness of your behaviors and the emotions you attach to them. Self-awareness leads to the management of your emotions and increases awareness of others.

In his book *Let Your Life Speak,* Parker Palmer (2000) identifies five skills that you can develop to support your inner work. These skills work well with the Cycles of Reflection.

1. Meditation

Parker Palmer (2000) describes meditation as the conscious act of calming the mind and body by focusing. Meditation is relaxing, improves concentration, and may increase your self-esteem. The simplest form of meditation involves taking a few focused breaths, which you can perform anytime at home or at work. One suggestion is to use a few moments of meditative breathing to focus yourself during a stressful situation. Taking short pauses to breathe during the work day will help you to get in touch with your physiology, emotions, and attitudes at the moment. This process can greatly assist you in choosing the best response to a situation, which will impact positively on the future. You must control your emotions if you wish to model good character. Here are a few examples of times when you can use a minute or two to meditate:

> Some people think that meditation takes time away from physical accomplishments. Taken to extreme, of course, that's true. Most people, however, find that meditation creates more time than it takes.
>
> —Peter McWilliams, author

- During a washroom break
- Just prior to taking a phone call
- While driving your car
- Just before students arrive to your class
- During student individual study or quiet reading
- While walking or driving to a meeting

2. Prayer

Palmer's (2000) second suggestion is prayer. You have the power to have whatever you desire in life, including at work. Taking a few moments through-

As long as there are tests, there will be prayer in schools.

—Anonymous

out each day to sit in a state of reflection gives you an opportunity to connect with your higher spirit, request guidance, and give thanks for what you have. If you are feeling sorry for yourself, you cannot behave in a way that creates a positive environment for others. Being able to give empathy, kindness, acceptance, and love comes out of living a spiritual life and being grateful for what you have. A "vision board" is a very powerful tool you can use to focus on the positive aspects of your life, as well as the goals that you desire. It can be made by simply collecting a group of pictures that represent what you want most in life, placing them onto a mat, and then posting them in a location where you can look at them everyday.

3. Journaling

Journaling is a valuable way to begin the process of self-reflection. There are many forms that journaling can take. Use your journal as a place to deposit ideas, theories, and random thoughts resulting from your daily observations. It's also a good place to identify your hopes, fears, and acknowledge your weaknesses and successes.

You may want to begin by keeping your journal on your night table beside your bed and responding to a set of questions or prompts that you have created to guide your reflections. At work, bring your journal to meetings, workshops, and conferences. If you are a teacher, make journaling part of a regular activity that you and your students engage in together.

Keep a journal and learn to see how you are as an individual.

—John Edwards, politician

It may be of value to make note of the date, time, and location for future reference.

Each day you receive insights about the way you are taking responsibility for your role as an educator. You must capture those kernels of wisdom and use them to make better choices in the future.

4. Reflective Reading

Reading is a very powerful example of a life experience. Reflective reading provides insights into the ideas, thoughts, theories, and experiences of other people. Reading by itself will not create the inner change you are looking for. However, by using reading, together with the other four skills in the Cycle of Reflection, you can actively practice responding to old situations in a new way. Reading for short periods of time each day will nurture your personal growth. Excellent times to read are first thing in the morning or last thing in the day. Reflective reading also inspires reflective journaling. Here are a few ways to incorporate reflective reading into the work day.

— ❧ —

To read without reflecting is like eating without digesting.

—Edmond Burke, British Philosopher

- Create a book study group with your colleagues.
- Read to your students.
- Share short sections from a book with a colleague.
- Start a book exchange or book club in the school.
- Include reading a book segment as part of the preparation for a meeting.
- Post quotes that inspire reflection in the classroom, common areas, offices, and meeting rooms.

5. Spiritual Friendship

The inner work that you engage in is very personal. However, that doesn't mean it needs to be private. When you share personal thoughts and feeling with a partner, you take responsibility for your imperfections. You become free to begin the outward journey that may leave you feeling vulnerable with others. Having the opportunity to share frustrations and fears can often dissolve emotions that might cause you to react negatively to a situation. Identify one colleague you know you can trust to listen, to know your darkest fears, to push you when you need

— ❧ —

One of the greatest moments in anybody's developing experience is when he no longer tries to hide from himself but determines to get acquainted with himself as he really is.

—Norman Vincent Peale, author

Figure 3.6   Cycle of Reflection With Inner Work

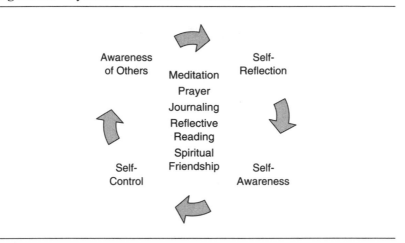

encouragement, and comfort you when you are feeling overextended. Plan to take short walks together or allow time for an evening phone call to share your experiences.

Making a personal commitment to doing the inner work by engaging in self-reflection, meditation, prayer, journaling, and spiritual friendship will connect you to the powerful lessons of personal experience (See Figure 3.6). Having a better understanding of yourself gives you a greater feeling of self-worth and increases your awareness of others. As a result, your ability to model good character while interacting with students and colleagues is enhanced.

THE SECOND E: THE POWER OF EXCHANGE

The Ramp

Huntsville High School has five sets of doors that provide access to the outside. Two of them lead out to a ramp bordering the town side of the school. One set of doors is at the top and the other set is at the bottom. The doors at the top of the ramp are used by students who are walking to and

> Communication is the exchange of information and feelings that leads to mutual understanding. Communication makes a bond or a connection between giver and receiver, between different departments, manager and staff, teacher and student.
>
> —Peter Urs Bender (1997)

from the downtown area before and after school and during the lunch period.

The ramp had been home for about 50 to 60 of the toughest kids we had at the school. Students went there to socialize, hide while skipping classes, gather for a good fight, and engage in other inappropriate activities. The ramp was a challenging situation to manage. The group at the top of ramp did not get along with the group at the bottom. Sometimes they would drift into each others' territory and a fight would break out. There could be 100 kids in a circle watching while two students were fighting. Often they weren't students. Because the ramp was so close to town, former students, students from other schools, dropouts, and drifters would come to the area looking to sell drugs, connect with a friend, or meet someone that they had their eye on.

The problem on the ramp was a situation that I grappled with for some time. When I became principal of the school, I wanted to solve the ramp problem. There had been a decrease in the number of fights, and many of the tougher kids I had confronted over the years had graduated or dropped out. So I felt the timing was right.

I started by going out to the students to talk with them about the situation. I wanted the students to understand that the behaviors that typically took place on the ramp for so many years were not acceptable to the school and the surrounding community. I called for a meeting between the administration, our community police officer, and all of the students who were using the ramp. During the meeting, I explained the concerns brought forward by staff, parents, and members of the community. We discussed the options that we had to resolve the problem. At first there was resistance. One student said I would never be successful in moving students off the ramp because "her father and her father's father grew up fighting on that ramp." Things got a little emotional at times, but I let them finish talking as long as they weren't rude or disrespectful. We had three meetings with the students over the next couple of weeks to continue our discussion and brainstorm solutions. Each time the students seemed a little more receptive to the idea of moving off the ramp. The turning point came when we agreed to create a new space where benches would be provided and the students could paint the area with artwork. The area was much more visible and allowed the staff to better supervise the students.

It was a wonderful warm spring day when we undertook the project of cleaning up the new area for kids to hang out and socialize. There was a lot of winter dirt and garbage to clean up. A boundary area was marked off with spray paint and heavy duty picnic tables, and garbage cans were moved into position and given a fresh coat of paint.

Students don't hang out on the ramp anymore. It's not the cool place to be. It took me seven years to find the courage to have the conversations needed with students to solve the ramp problem. During that time, I had focused on suspending students instead of modeling a solution to the problem.

The Process of Mutual Influence

In the first section of this chapter, I discussed how to learn from the power of your experiences. Experiences can influence your self-esteem, which can affect your sense of vulnerability and ability to model good character. The next focus will be on modeling good character through the power of exchange.

We must purposely address the importance of harmonious relationships and model values inherent in good relationships with students and staff.

—Ashley Zabel

Students, teachers, and principals are continually engaged in the process of influencing each other by exchanging knowledge, ideas, and viewpoints for the purpose of teaching and learning. Figure 3.7, Relationships Based on Power and Authority, illustrates an unbalanced exchange of information between

Figure 3.7   Relationships Based on Power and Authority

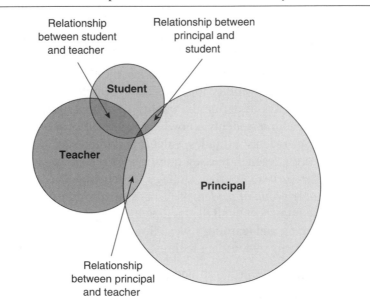

the student, teacher, and principal where the relationships are influenced by the power and authority traditionally held by the principal.

In Figure 3.7, the size of the circle represents the amount of power and authority that the principal, teacher, and student respectively have during the exchange process. By power and authority, I am referring to the amount of information and decision-making authority each of them has over the other. The intersecting areas define the amount of mutual influence in each relationship, including the area intersected by all three individuals. In an unbalanced relationship, principals have the greatest amount of authority. However, their degree of mutual influence over teachers and students is less than what exists between the teacher and the student. The mutual influence among all three is very low. This is a typical scenario in many schools. Regardless, the teacher and principal have a responsibility to model behaviors that build trusting relationships with others, such as listening, empathy, risk taking, and respect.

Factors Affecting Quality Relationships

———————— ✂ ————————

Learning of students' interests outside the classroom is one way to show students I care about them. Knowing their interests will ultimately help me understand them better.

—Jessica Davis

A recent study conducted by researcher Holfve-Sabel (2006) in Sweden examined students' attitudes toward their teachers. She found that students' attitude and how they felt about their teacher affected their behavior and ability to learn in the classroom environment. This study supports a connection between the teacher modeling certain behaviors and the students' ability to learn. The researcher concluded that there are two ways to define the quality of schooling: first, by the improvement in the students' knowledge and skills, and second, by the change in students' attitudes, values, and interests.

If you are a teacher, the key question you must ask yourself is, "What is the *most* appropriate strategy for teaching this material *to this particular group of students?*" To answer the question, you will need to take into account all the factors affecting your students, such as prior learning and learning styles. However, you will also need to find out how your students are feeling about your class. For example

- How do the students feel about their relationship with you?
- How do the students feel about the classroom environment?

- How do the students feel about their relationships with their peers?
- How do the students feel about the subject?

As a principal, you have similar questions to consider when determining the most appropriate strategies for influencing teachers and their interests and attitudes toward modeling good character.

The answers to these questions will lead to a better understanding of the needs of your

The mere act of greeting students at the door instead of sitting at the desk can set the tone for the whole school year, if not more.

—Maryse Daitch,
teacher at San Dieguito Academy

students and colleagues and which behaviors to model to influence their beliefs, attitudes, and behaviors. Teachers who seek to understand by answering questions, like the ones above, have a greater capacity to model caring, trust, and mutual influence. "Teachers are the brokers of caring schools" (Bosworth, 1995; Bosworth & Ferreira, 2000). Figure 3.8, Relationships of Mutual Influence, illustrates a balanced exchange of information between the student, teacher, and principal.

Figure 3.8   Relationships of Mutual Influence

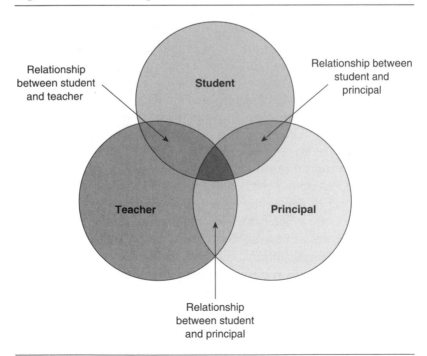

The principal, teacher, and student share equally in the exchange of information and the process of decision making. Balancing power and authority increases the opportunity for mutual influence by meeting the needs of each person. As a principal, modeling this for your teachers will demonstrate to them caring and nurture trusting relationships. As a teacher, balancing power and authority in your classroom can have a significant influence on how your students are feeling, also influencing their beliefs, attitudes, and behaviors.

Modeling Courageous Conversations

———————— ✥ ————————

We can teach a lot of things, but if we can't relate to a group of friendly students, you will never be a competent teacher.

—William Glasser, psychiatrist

The way you feel about yourself affects the quality of your relationships with your students, colleagues, and principal. The next section examines how modeling courageous conversations will help you improve communication and build relationships of mutual influence. Courageous conversations are those conversations where individuals take responsibility for sharing how they feel about a situation in an honest, caring, compassionate, and respectful way.

I have been an elementary and secondary teacher, department head, guidance counselor, principal, and committee and conference chair. Those roles have provided me with many powerful experiences that have shaped my identity and ability to build relationships. You may be teaching English with the aim of improving your students' literacy skills. If you are an intermediate division curriculum leader, you may be assigned the responsibility of reviewing common strategies for instructional planning with other Grade 7 and 8 teachers. Convening a regional track and field meet may be one of your volunteer duties as the track and field coach. If you are the principal, you are responsible for completing teacher performance appraisals. To be successful, you must work with others, have the ability to exchange information, and build quality relationships. Think about the times you were calling parents to discuss a problem concerning their child. Did it stress you out? Speaking with others can involve a lot of risk taking.

Figure 3.9, Modeling Courageous Conversations, illustrates five strategies you can use to model courageous conversation.

Figure 3.9   Modeling Courageous Conversations

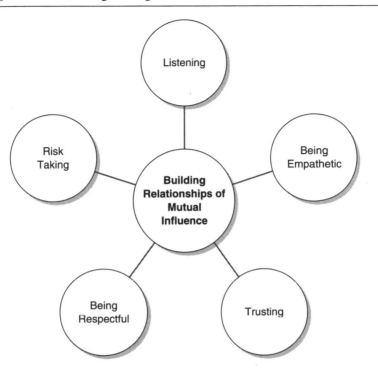

Each day you have hundreds of conversations you may take for granted, never listening carefully enough to understand the other person's feelings or point of view. Self-monitoring what and how you speak can significantly change how you behave with others and influence how they feel about the quality of relationship they have with you. Modeling the skills used in courageous conversations can also influence the behavior of others. Conversation is the most important tool you have to assist in building quality relationships and modeling good character. Here are five skills that can be developed to model courageous conversations.

1. Listening

In *The Seven Habits of Highly Effective People,* Stephen Covey (2004) coined the phrase *seek first to understand.* Good listening results in a better understanding of the other person's thoughts and feelings. When someone is speaking to you, stop and suspend all other activity. Stay focused by maintaining eye contact, listening to

———————— ✧ ————————

You cannot truly listen to anyone and do anything else at the same time.

—M. Scott Peck, author

the tone of voice, and watching for body language. When the person is finished talking, try to pause for a moment before responding. Be aware of your own inner voice and try to control your emotional response to the other person's ideas and opinions. Ask questions and restate the main idea back to the person. If you are a principal, provide an opportunity for teachers to share ideas in a more formal setting. One strategy for principals is to open up their inner circle of advisors to include a variety of teachers. If you are a teacher, try structuring regular classroom meetings to give students an opportunity to express their views on matters concerning their learning environment. Here are a few important guidelines for listening:

- Don't jump to conclusions about the person's ideas.
- Time invested in listening at the beginning will save you time in the end.
- Listening gives you leverage when negotiating.
- Active listening shows other people that you care about their ideas and feelings.

2. Being Empathetic

Having empathy allows you to understand the feelings that others are experiencing in various situations. You must be in touch with your feelings before you can accept the feelings of others. Compassion and sensitivity go hand in hand with being empathetic and are important when building trust with your students and colleagues.

Showing empathy in a conversation can be particularly helpful when there is a disagreement or when hearing a complaint from

———————— ✧ ————————

If you can't have empathy, and have effective relationships, no matter how smart you are, you are not going to get very far.

—Daniel Goleman, author

others. Take the position that each staff and student concern you receive is very real to them. The power of empathy is illustrated in a study that showed that teacher disposition of caring and empathy is a strong indicator of improved student performance in reading and math (Helm, 2007).

3. Being Respectful

Respect is our first moral mission (Lickona, 1991). It requires that you treat yourself and others as inherently having value and is necessary for building caring interpersonal relationships. Showing respect during conversations involves listening and validating the thoughts and feelings of others. Knowing how to listen without being judgemental or defensive gives others the opportunity to solve their own problems without the need for unsolicited advice. Using common courtesies like please and thank you shows respect for another person.

4. Trusting

It is important to always speak the truth or say nothing at all. Individuals often have the need to say something false because they fear they may have to say the truth.

There are numerous trust relationships that exist in your school environment. In *Leadership in Empowered Schools,* Paula Short and John Greer (1997) suggest that trust begins with the principal. The principal engages in many conversations with staff throughout the course of a working day. Much time is devoted to fielding questions and making decisions. To nurture trust, the principal must share authority by delegating responsibility to others. The trust among teachers comes from working collaboratively on issues affecting school.

> My attitude and behavior toward my students and the way I structure my classroom will have an important effect on my students' self-concept.
>
> —Anna Dioguardi,
> staff member (Beyond Borders)

5. Risk Taking

In a school environment that encourages risk taking and innovation, principals, teachers, and students share ideas in a freethinking atmosphere. The idea of freethinking suggests participating in dialogue without the fear of ridicule or taking matters personally. You can take responsibility for your own risk taking by allowing yourself to be vulnerable when speaking with others. It is one of the most powerful ways of improving

> Every working moment in an educator's day, through conduct and attitude, is sending out a moral message (Kristjannson, 2006).

communication and building quality relationships. Don't be afraid to reveal yourself. If you make a mistake, simply admit it. If you don't understand, ask for help. Colleagues will prefer and value your honesty. Authentic communication shows courage and builds integrity.

You are under the watchful eye of those that surround you. If you want to model good character you need to monitor what you say and do. Simple things, like your body language and tone of voice, can demonstrate caring and trust. By continuing to do inner work and applying good communication skills in your conversations with others, you slowly build quality relationships of mutual influence. Building quality relationships with your students, principal, parents, and colleagues requires modeling good communication.

THE THIRD E: THE POWER OF EMPOWERMENT

The Role of the Principal

———————— ✤ ————————

If we believe there is only one right way—our way—then those who are different must be wrong.

—Peter Urs Bender (1997)

———————— ✤ ————————

Just when I'm ready to retire, I'm beginning to learn what this job is all about.

—Anonymous principal
after 30 years of service

The principal is someone who has the power to cast a shadow or project a light onto some part of the world and onto the lives of the people who live there (Palmer, 2000). When principals model good character, they affect the feelings that others have toward those in a position of leadership and authority. Building trust in schools requires the principal to empower teachers. Therefore, to empower teachers, it is extremely important that principals model good character in all they do with faculty and students.

What makes up the inner and outer world of a school principal, and what behaviors must you, as principal, model to encourage teacher involvement in schoolwide matters?

The Inner World of the Principal: Self-Empowerment

Deciding exactly what a good school looks like and how to create it are significant challenges for principals. Teachers become principals because they have strong feelings about what a good school should be and have a desire to bring about the required changes. Therefore, they are highly motivated to meet the challenge. The desire to make change may also be affected by feelings associated with control, power, and personal identity. Awareness of these feelings, and how you as principal choose to control them, is a test of self-confidence and commitment to building quality relationships. Before discussing strategies that principals can use to encourage teacher involvement, here are five obstacles principals must overcome to control their emotions.

> We can easily forgive a child that is afraid of the dark. The real tragedy of life is when an adult is afraid of the light.
>
> —Plato

> Inviting teachers to pursue anything they lack passion for is encouraging them to invest in frustration and guilt.
>
> —Richard Sagor (2005)

1. Insecurity

How many of you are principals whose identity is wrapped up in your job? There are many demands placed on you each day. If you are insecure about who you are, you may experience feelings of self-doubt and a lack of self-worth. Your feelings of success may hinge on your sense of responsibility to get it right. To overcome these feelings, you must strive to give up some of the responsibility for the decisions that determine the future of the school.

2. Believing the World Is a Battleground

The road to becoming a principal is both political and competitive. Once you are there, the fight to stay on top is even fiercer. Standardized testing, and school-by-school comparing of results, can push you to focus exclusively on strategies that will result in greater student achievement. One way to counter this pressure is to shift the focus from achievement to support. You can adopt the belief that teachers are professionals, and given an opportunity to work in an environment of trust, they will do their best to help students succeed. You can also create high quality working conditions for your teachers. Teacher working conditions are student learning conditions.

3. Believing in Ultimate Responsibility

Research shows that a principal makes approximately 56 decisions every hour. Being like most principals, you are an extrovert by nature, so you often feel compelled to fix every problem and make every decision that is presented to you. By doing so, you are imposing your will upon others. Slowing down long enough to reflect on the best response to each decision is a challenge. One of the most powerful strategies you can use to slow the decision-making process down is to ask yourself the following two questions:

- Can this decision be made at some other time?
- Is there someone else who is responsible for, and capable of, making this decision?

If the answer to both of these questions is yes, then you are not responsible for responding immediately with a solution to the problem. The person needing an answer likely has a solution and can take responsibility for the decision. Your role will be to provide guidance with respect to timelines and the necessary resources required to support the solution.

—— ❧ ——

No man is fit to command another that cannot command himself.

—William Penn

4. Fear of Failure

Principals work hard to create structures that will ensure order, reduce disorganization, streamline operations, and eliminate surprises. In terms of managing a school, this can have many positive benefits. However, these structures can also be used by principals to avoid conflict and situations that require making difficult or unpopular decisions. If your identity and sense of self-worth are closely connected to achieving success, then your fear of failure may discourage creativity, innovation, and prevent you from adopting structures and processes that nurture empowerment.

5. Denial

In his book *Let Your Life Speak: Listening for the Voice of Vocation,* Parker Palmer (2000) talks about the fact that for many leaders denial is very closely linked to the fear of failure. Do you refuse to let go of situations that aren't working? Are you afraid to give an idea the time it may need to come to fruition? To answer these two questions you need to examine your drive to take responsibility for everything. Accepting failure as a natural part of learning means you will never have to hide your mistakes from staff. Your willingness to listen to the voice of others will provide you with everything you need to make better decisions in the future.

> Death is not the biggest fear we have; our biggest fear is taking the risk to be alive . . . the risk to be alive and express what we really are.
>
> —Don Miguel Ruiz (1997)

The Outer World of the Principal—Empowering Teachers

"How and what administrators communicate is critical to forming the nurturing and empowering relationships necessary for teachers to risk change and teach most effectively" (Laud, 1998). Ensuring that honesty and integrity are part of all aspects of communications is the key to ensuring success (Bender, 1997).

> Teacher empowerment requires investing in teachers the right to participate in the determination of school goals and policies, and the right to exercise professional judgement about the content of the curriculum and the means of instruction.
>
> —Blase and Blase (1994)

Modeling a Vision

Before I started my first day as principal of Huntsville High School, I wanted to be clear in my own mind about what my priorities were for the school. I needed to know this for three reasons.

> I want to be a good role model to my teachers so they see healthy relational values. I want them to know that I deeply care about them.
>
> —Jan Olsson

- I wanted to make a statement to the faculty about what I valued most in my role as principal.
- I needed a guideline for how I was going to use my time and energy.
- I wanted to be prepared to respond when teachers asked me questions about where I stood on school matters.

Figure 3.10, Principal's Vision for Huntsville High School, shows the vision statement that I presented to teachers, secretaries, educational assistants, and custodial staff at my first faculty meeting.

As I was developing the vision statement, I remember saying to myself, "I don't want to commit to too much. I want to leave lots of opportunity for teachers to decide what needs to happen next." I convinced myself that modeling this strategy would create a positive result. The vision statement focused on structures and processes that would empower staff. I believe that the vision, though still a work in progress, has served its purpose. It made a statement to staff that *how* we accomplished our goals together was just as important as *what* we accomplished. It prepared me to respond to the many questions staff had regarding schoolwide matters.

Here are four structures and processes that will nurture empowerment.

1. Effective Communication

Effective communication requires the use of a variety of structures such as staff meetings, conferences, written memos, and formal

Figure 3.10   Principal's Vision for Huntsville High School

Principal's Vision
for
Huntsville
High School:
Identify and Implement
Structures and Processes
That Will
Inspire and Support
Effective Communication,
Shared Decision Making,
Innovation, and
Celebration.

conferences with individual teachers (Blase & Kirby, 1992). The following list of suggestions will assist you in improving your communication skills. They focus on the *process* of communicating. And they will work for teachers too!

- Model effective communication by consistently aligning yourself with the school vision and what you expect from the teaching staff.
- Communication can be verbal or nonverbal. You know your ability to use self-reflection will assist you in becoming aware of the image you are projecting to others. For example, it is very important to understand the impact your body language can have on teacher perception.
- Spend less time giving advice and more time listening to what others have to say. (This is one of my challenges.) Increased time spent reading, listening, and observing will help you receive information about how others are feeling.
- Make being visible a day-to-day priority.
- Filter all written and verbal communication for clarity. Be sure to separate fact from opinion. Provide clear explanations for your ideas and check for understanding with the receiver.
- Express differences of opinion without being confrontational.
- Display sensitivity for the differences and needs of other groups and individuals.

> Speech is power: Speech is to persuade, to convert, to compel. It is to bring another out of his bad sense into your good sense.
>
> —Ralph Waldo Emerson, philosopher

2. Shared Decision Making

Developing a school culture of collaboration will increase teacher involvement around many important school matters (Lumsden, 1998; Short & Greer, 1997). Here are several suggestions you can use to encourage more collaboration in your school:

- Create a problem-solving team by bringing a small group of faculty together to brainstorm solutions to a schoolwide issue or concern. The simple process of coming together and then putting into action those solutions can empower teachers.

———————— ✧ ————————

The truth is that many people set rules to keep from making decisions.

—Mike Krzyzewski,
NCAA basketball coach

- When teachers ask for information that affects schoolwide matters such as budget and timetabling, be transparent. If you can't share, then let them know why.

- Communicate an open invitation to all staff to bring forward opinions and solutions to problems.
- Provide opportunities for teachers to make decisions for themselves and then support those decisions openly.

3. Risk Taking and Innovation

Schools form part of a complex educational system designed for teaching and learning. Schools are also part of a larger bureaucracy, and a significant number of rules and regulations control what can and can't be done on a day-to-day basis. Nothing frustrates teachers more than the inability to change the conditions under which they must teach. Your goal is to inspire innovation in your school. Innovation requires adaptability, autonomy, openness to change, and opportunities for empowerment. Here are a few key tips to foster innovation.

———————— ✧ ————————

If the conditions of work are such that it is unreasonable for a person to expect success, then pessimism, alienation, and burnout should be expected.

—Richard Sagor (2005)

- Know the needs of your school community. Look for opportunities to make change and then share with teachers your passion and commitment to become involved.
- Model risk taking.
- As suggested previously, create problem-solving teams to brainstorm solutions to schoolwide problems and issues.
- Encourage conversations that focus on trying new ideas.
- Publicly reward innovation.

4. Celebration and Praise

Giving praise is one of the most effective ways to motivate teachers and influence their beliefs, attitudes, and behavior (Blase &

Kirby, 1992). It can also be very rewarding for you. Here are a few suggestions, identified by teachers and supported by research, on the best way to celebrate and praise teachers.

—————— ❦ ——————

I can live for two months on a good compliment.

—Mark Twain

- Praise sincerely in congruence with your other behavior.
- Maximize your use of nonverbal communication through the use of smiles, nods, and touches.
- Schedule time for teacher recognition during faculty meetings, public announcements, and assemblies. Show pride in your teachers.
- Write brief personal notes to compliment people.
- Praise briefly.
- Tie praise to specific achievements and professional accomplishments.

Some Final Thoughts

The importance and impact of teachers and principals modeling good character cannot be overstated. Reflecting on your experiences can strengthen your self-esteem and assist you in nurturing quality relationships of mutual influence with your students and colleagues. Effective communication is the tool you will use to model good character and empower others.

Creating harmony between who you are and the work you do can bring meaning, fulfilment, and contentment to each day. The behaviors that teachers and the principal model can affect a student's attitudes, motivations, expectations, behaviors, and desire to learn. To accomplish this, you must commit to modeling the behavior that you expect to see in your students. From my experiences, modeling is the most difficult thing we do as educators because we can't really blame anyone else for our own behaviors. I encourage you to reflect on your values and the way they influence your behavior with students and colleagues. Though a challenging process, the rewards of personal growth and modeling, both personally and professionally, are many. There is always enough time to grow.

QUOTES

Teaching, like any truly human activity, emerges from one's inwardness, for better or for worse.

—Parker Palmer (1998),
The Courage to Teach

The true teacher defends his pupils against his own personal influences.

—Amos Alcott,
teacher and writer

The warmth of the school, the constant interaction between students and teachers, even in informal settings, and the positive feelings that existed between staff members and the principal all created the impression of a school that truly knew its role and purpose.

—Paula Short and John Greer (1997),
Leadership Empowered Schools

CHAPTER FOUR

Establishing Rules and Procedures for Civility

Creating a Positive School and Classroom Environment

Achieving our academic goals will require a civil climate that will enhance the teacher's opportunity to teach, as well as a child's opportunity to learn.

—Philip Fitch Vincent (2005)

INTRODUCTION

Students who develop good character have been given the opportunity to practice over and over the socially appropriate responses to a variety of situations, until those specific behaviors are engraved in their personality (Vincent, 1999). For example, in schools we want our students to act responsibly, which is considered by our society as a mark of good character. Responsibility comes from three words: *re*—meaning over and over; *sponse*—meaning to respond; and *ability*—meaning the capacity to do. Students become responsible citizens by practicing over and over the appropriate response to specific situations, such as being on time for class and completing homework assignments. If the students don't meet the school's expectations for appropriate behavior, it becomes very difficult to establish an orderly environment where teachers can teach and students can learn. And so a comprehensive character development program must identify appropriate student behaviors (such as being responsible), clearly define the school's expectations, and create opportunities for students to practice the right behavior.

According to University of Louisville Professor Dr. Terry Scott (personal communication, 2006), behavior is the most difficult issue that teachers face on a day-to-day basis. Disrespect, noncompliance, and simple disruptions are the most time consuming and frequent challenges for teachers and administrators. A lack of university preparation for dealing with problem behaviors amplifies the problem.

According to Dr. Philip Fitch Vincent (2005), schools traditionally have little difficulty establishing rules for proper etiquette. The principal's address to the student body at the first assembly, posted rules in the hallways, and a class-by-class review of the school code of behavior are all important strategies that communicate the rules of a school. However, student compliance may be short-lived unless all staff and students are given the opportunity to develop the rules *and* the procedures required to follow them. Then the opportunity to subsequently practice the steps or procedures that will reinforce the appropriate behavior will be required to successfully teach the desired behavior.

The support of a *safe and inviting physical environment* will provide the foundation for compliance. Students' impressions of their learning environment including teacher skill, feelings about school maintenance, if their school is a good school, whether issues exist (such as bullying), all contribute to student compliance. The most important idea to keep at the forefront of your mind is that promoting character development goes beyond the establishing and enforcement of rules. A student's feeling of a lack of connection to the staff, resulting when rule enforcement takes priority over relationship building, may have a negative effect on the success of teaching good character to students (Evans, 2008).

Chapters 2 and 3 identified *safe and inviting physical environment* and *staff modeling good character* as two foundational components of a simple and real character development framework for schools. This chapter will outline the third component of the framework, *rules and procedures for civility,* shown in Figure 4.1.

The successful implementation of these three foundational components forms a character development threshold that ensures that students and teachers are working together in a mutually respectful

Figure 4.1   Rules and Procedures for Civility

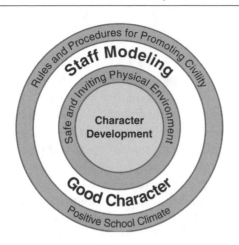

Source: Trillium Lakelands District School Board, Ontario, Canada. Reprinted with permission.

educational environment. Schools that have a safe, caring, and orderly learning environment, based on relationships of mutual respect, are well positioned to deliver a curriculum that further enhances learning and the development of good character in their students.

What are the most effective approaches to character-based discipline? How effective are consequences compared to positive reinforcement? Where and when is discipline most effectively applied by teachers and administrators? Let's look at the answers to these and other questions.

THE NEED FOR DISCIPLINE IN ESTABLISHING A POSITIVE SCHOOL CLIMATE

The Deer Carcass

One warm and sunny spring afternoon, I was looking through the office window toward the patio at the front of our school. I saw a student violently kicking at the doors leading into the cafeteria. As

> As the school climate of caring and civility grows, a safe and orderly environment should evolve and academic achievement will rise.
>
> —Philip Fitch Vincent (2005)

I watched I noticed something hanging from the door. It appeared to be the carcass of an animal. It actually turned out to be the hind quarters of a deer. Three senior students, who were skipping class, had been out in the bush on a trail ride in their pickup truck. They had come across a deer carcass—the remains of a wolf kill. They decided to load the carcass into the back of the pickup and bring it to school to play a practical joke. The legs were used to barricade the cafeteria doors so that no student could get out of the building. It didn't take me much effort to determine who was responsible because I had one of the boys in my sights. News of the event spread quickly throughout the school. Teachers and students were very upset.

In society there are consequences for inappropriate behaviors. Laws governing those behaviors are established and reviewed, in an ongoing fashion, by legislators and the courts. Because schools mirror society, it is important for schools to examine which behaviors are appropriate, and not appropriate, based on the attributes determined by the school and supporting community.

The deer carcass story is very unique. In terms of consequences, the solution seemed pretty straight forward to me. Each student responsible for bringing the dead animal parts back to the school would be suspended. Perhaps the students should write a letter of apology to staff and students and spend some time with the custodians working on the building. However, in this particular situation, the parents of the offending students were not supportive. They did not view the actions of their children as being wrong, in poor moral character, or creating a potential health risk. The parents' lack of support made for some challenging discussions. Regardless, consequences were levied and the rules of civility for our school were reinforced.

The deer carcass story demonstrates that disciplining in today's world is a complex task. It requires open communication and a willingness to use discipline as an opportunity to educate.

Civility in the Common Areas of the School

Addressing student behavior in the common areas of the school, such as respectful language, consideration for others' personal space, and kindness toward those with visible and nonvisible challenges, may be the most effective approach to fostering a civil school climate. Developing consistency in schoolwide expectations and disciplinary practices in these areas, when combined with effective classroom management, will provide the appropriate boundaries for students (Marzano, 2003).

There are several reasons why it may be best to begin building school civility in the common areas.

—————— ⚛ ——————

Changes in student behavior in the common areas of the school have a direct impact on student behavior inside the classroom.

—Jan Olsson

- Teachers are more comfortable dealing with the common areas. Until a foundation of trust is established, teachers may have difficulty discussing their classroom management issues with others.
- Each classroom may be managed in a slightly different way with little impact on the whole-school climate.
- It's easier to collect data in the common areas and, therefore, receive feedback on the efforts being made to change student behavior and develop good character.
- Students see the staff as presenting a united front.

Responding to inappropriate student behavior is a challenging and time consuming effort for educators. The following two theories will provide strategies for responding to schoolwide behaviors in an efficient and effective manner.

The Bubble Theory

A school's student body is made up of a number of smaller social groupings of students. These groupings are often unique unto themselves. The students within each grouping may be connected with each other because of similar interests, such as participation on an athletic team or student council. They may group themselves through other associated behaviors, such as truancy or illegal activity such as trafficking drugs. Adolescents are highly social and at a point in their development when their connections to others help define who they are, which motivates them to group together.

If you are a principal or vice principal and spend a good portion of your day walking around your school, you can easily identify these groupings, who the students are, where in the school they congregate, and what behaviors they tend to exhibit. These behaviors are a reflection of the beliefs and attitudes that form part of the students' character.

If you think of each of these groupings as a bubble, then it is possible to develop a schoolwide discipline strategy that monitors and responds to issues that originate from any number of these social groupings throughout the school. Figure 4.2, The Bubble Theory, conceptualizes a schoolwide organization of social groupings based on these student interests and behaviors.

Each bubble represents a grouping of students with common interest. The Ss in each circle are the students. These groups are typically six to eight individuals in size. Groups may be smaller or larger. Each group of students, given their makeup, may present their own unique characteristic behaviors. Some groups are well behaved, others to a lesser degree. Each group will have one or two leaders that model the accepted behavior for that particular group. The Ls in each circle represent the leaders.

The underlying premise behind the bubble theory is that it is difficult to respond to every inappropriate behavior that occurs in a school. Much like controlling speeding on our highways, a systematic approach to monitoring and responding to behavior may be more effective. There are a number of strategies that support the implementation of the theory:

- Know the bubbles intimately—where they are located, who is in them, who the leader is, and the predominant behavior of the group.

Figure 4.2   The Bubble Theory

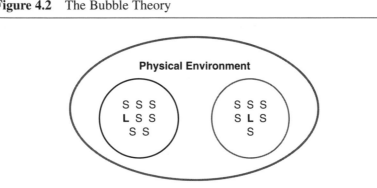

- Establish a positive and ongoing relationship with each group, including the leader.
- Focus on the problem groups first.
- Increase adult presence around the problem groups.
- Provide an incentive to recalcitrant groups to conform and become engaged in the school through positive reinforcement and modifying the physical environment.
- Give challenging groups of students a reason to move to a more appropriate setting by changing some aspect of the physical environment.
- If necessary, use logical consequences with the leader for inappropriate behavior.
- The closest followers in the group may also need to be given a consequence for inappropriate behavior.

The Bubble Theory supports a systematic approach to monitoring and responding to the behaviors of various student groups throughout the common areas of the school. The theory provides a system for applying a combination of proactive and preventative measures and consequences. From my personal experience, adult visibility, a smiling face, and a caring comment can have a positive impact on most groups of students.

The Mountain Theory

In schools with a large student population, tracking and responding to every display of poor character can be a challenge. Contractual constraints such as the ratio of administrators in a building, particularly the number of vice principals assigned to a large middle or secondary school, and the supervision minutes assigned to teachers, may impact on the school's ability to maintain a civil environment. A systematic plan that focuses teacher and principal time on task can balance workload and allow for an effective response to unacceptable student behavior.

Figure 4.3, The Mountain Theory, illustrates the typical pattern of inappropriate student behaviors in a school.

The Mountain Theory, like the Bubble Theory, supports the development of a system for tracking and responding to inappropriate behavior. Given a chosen population of students, for any particular misbehavior, there will likely be a large number of students who display the behavior only on occasion, if at all. Those students are identified as Section A. At the top of the mountain, there will be a much smaller group of students who display the same behavior much more frequently. These students are identified in Section C. The individuals in Section B display the behavior; however, it may not be chronic as of yet. Implementing a response system using the Mountain Theory requires defining a target-size group of noncompliant students and developing a strategy for changing the behavior.

Let's use attendance at the secondary school level, specifically truancy, as an example. A principal or vice principal responsible for attendance will want to get to truant students quickly by using a progressive discipline model, as outlined later in this chapter, that acts as a deterrent for those who are considering skipping class. The first area of focus must be Section A at the base of the mountain, often representing young students who are experimenting with skipping

Figure 4.3   The Mountain Theory

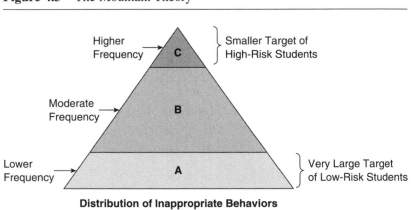

class but haven't developed the habit yet. In a middle or secondary school, focusing interventions on the students in the younger grades may prevent the increased prevalence of a certain behavior, like truancy, in the future. The goal is to prevent Section A students from becoming a Section B statistic by assisting them with developing the habit of regular and responsible attendance—an important part of their character development.

In terms of tracking attendance, Section C, at the top of the mountain, becomes the second target group. Students in Section C are chronically truant. They may also be involved in other behaviors that may impact on the climate of the school. They may encourage others to skip class. If they roam the building unsupervised, this may contribute to a rise in graffiti, vandalism, bullying, theft, and the disruption of classes in progress.

From a strategic point of view, the question becomes, where do you draw the two lines that define the categories of students? That may depend on your time, energy, commitment, determination, and resiliency. However, it is important to establish the target size of each group and then set forth a plan to engage those students. Continuing to look at the example of attendance, most school-based computer student-administration software programs will provide you with the data you will need to track attendance according to the criteria that you establish. Other behaviors, such as disrespectful language, may need to be tracked using a manual system that will be discussed later in this chapter.

Engaging Students in Common Areas

Staff willingness to engage students in the common areas is a sign of a healthy school culture. Principals and teachers need to be visible and modeling and practicing the skills of approaching students in a manner that is more likely to defuse a situation and nurture cooperation and compliance, rather than escalating the behavior. Here are several tips for engaging students in common areas such as the lunchroom or hallway:

- Use a soft voice.
- Ask to speak to the student in private.

- Refuse to get into a debate or justification for making a request.
- If necessary, walk away while indicating a time and place to meet.
- If you are a teacher, and the student refused to meet in private, report the uncooperative student to the office.
- Avoid large crowds without support.
- Maintain a calm disposition at all times, even in challenging situations.
- Positively reinforce good behavior.

PROGRESSIVE DISCIPLINE

Progressive Discipline

The situations where inappropriate behaviors occur are often complex. Think back to the deer carcass story. There may be different points of view, accounts of the facts, and opinions about what mitigating circumstances contributed to the situation. Such feelings may arise when teachers and administration rely too heavily on rule enforcement rather than relationship building. Developing a progressive discipline plan provides a guideline for approaching schoolwide discipline and the responses that the student, teacher, principal, and parent can anticipate.

> Most educators recognize the need for accountability and, if necessary, consequences for students that continually choose to disrupt the learning environment.
>
> —Dr. David Waangard
> (quoted in Vincent, 2005)

Progressive discipline is a whole-school approach that utilizes a continuum of interventions, supports, and consequences to address inappropriate student behaviors and builds on strategies that promote civil habits and the development of character traits such as honesty, responsibility for one's actions, and kindness. When inappropriate behavior occurs, disciplinary measures should be applied within a framework that shifts the focus from one that is solely punitive to one that is both corrective and supportive. Schools should utilize a range of interventions, supports, and consequences that include learning opportunities for reinforcing positive behavior while helping students to make good choices (Ontario Ministry of Education, 2007).

A progressive discipline approach to responding to inappropriate student behavior ensures that all possible actions and resources are utilized to improve that student's behavior. Ontario Ministry of Education Policy Memorandum 145, titled *Progressive Discipline and Promoting Positive Student Behavior* (2007), emphasizes the importance of combining discipline with education. Providing an appropriate and timely intervention, support, and consequence are part of a comprehensive view of the discipline process. An intervention may include implementing programs such as bullying prevention or citizenship development. A support strategy might include referring the student to an outside agency for counseling.

Detentions and suspensions are examples of consequences that may be initiated for certain behaviors. In some circumstances, short-term suspension may be a useful tool. In the case of a serious incident, long-term suspension or expulsion, which is further along the continuum of progressive discipline, may be the consequence that is required. For students with special education needs, interventions, supports, and consequences must be consistent with the student's strengths, needs, goals, and expectations contained within the student's Individual Education Plan.

When addressing inappropriate behavior, the following three points should be considered:

1. The particular student and personal circumstances

2. The nature and severity of the behavior

3. The impact of the behavior on school climate and safety

Chapter 3 discussed the importance of staff modeling good character. During the process of disciplining a student, teachers and principals must be conscientious of modeling good character via their communication. Regardless of the nature or severity of the inappropriate behavior, the adult's goal must always be to maintain the integrity of the child during the disciplining process.

Each school should create a progressive discipline model that guides the whole school. Figure 4.4, Progressive Discipline, outlines the progressive discipline model for Huntsville High School. The model is continually under review and revision.

In addition to following the steps in the model, guidelines have been established for staff and administration responsibilities as follows.

Staff Responsibilities

1. Conduct a classroom meeting to establish rules and procedures around lateness, cell phones, and other behavioral expectations.

Figure 4.4   Progressive Discipline

Huntsville High School Classroom Management

Progressive Discipline

STEP 1 THE CLASSROOM MEETING

- Establishing classroom rules and procedures
- Building moral democracy
- Maintenance

STEP 2 FIRST OFFENSE

- Verbal reminder
- Giving the "hairy eyeball"
- Moving into student's proximity

STEP 3 SECOND OFFENSE

- Brief conference with student outside the classroom

STEP 4 THIRD OFFENSE

- Brief conference with the student outside the classroom followed up with a teacher-student meeting at some other time
- Possible consequence (i.e., apology to the class, detention)
- Call home to the parent with direct contact

STEP 5 FOURTH OFFENSE

- Office referral
- Administration consequences—possible consequences includes restitution, reconciliation, counseling, various other interventions and supports, community service, suspension

---

2. Commit to Steps 1 through 4 of the Progressive Discipline Model. Specifically, record target behavior on the database, provide a consequence if needed, and call home.

3. Adopt the philosophy outlined in Figure 4.5, Maintaining Civility.

4. Have your classroom open each morning and before classes in order to clear the hallway.

Administration Responsibilities

1. Communicate to the student body the expectations for behavior.

2. Commit to Step 5 of the Progressive Discipline Model; specifically provide a consequence (i.e., cafeteria duty or detention for office referrals).

3. Adopt the philosophy outlined in Figure 4.5, Maintaining Civility.

4. Model the target behavior.

We will make every effort to proactively communicate our expectations to students and parents through the use of the school's Web site, newsletter, announcements, posters, and the support of Positive Behavior Intervention and Supports (PBIS), which will be discussed later in this chapter. At Huntsville High School, these messaging strategies are an important part of what we do as a staff to communicate our expectation.

The Classroom Meeting: Creating a Democratic Classroom Environment

In their 2000 book *Classrooms That Work: A Teacher's Guide to Discipline Without Stress*, Stan Shapiro and Karen Skinulis identify the classroom meeting as being at the core of a democratic approach to classroom discipline. Students need to be involved in the decisions that effect their learning environment. It doesn't mean that students will get to make decisions on rules and procedures that the teacher has decided on already. Some rules are nonnegotiable. However, the classroom meeting does provide an opportunity for students to express their opinions and suggestions, a forum for solving class problems, and an opportunity for input into the planning of their curriculum.

Shapiro and Skinulis (2000) suggest that the first week of instruction be given to developing the rules and procedures for civility, which includes the rules of meeting as a class. In subsequent weeks, time should be set aside to discuss with the students the progress of the class. A typical agenda might include positive feedback, classroom planning, review of responsibilities, problem solving, and personal problems.

The teacher has a significant role to play in building a positive relationship with students by establishing a positive classroom climate, creating a democratic class environment that includes interventions and supports, and establishing consequences for inappropriate behaviors. Teachers who embrace this approach to teaching take responsibility for the development of their students' character.

First Offense: Using the Space Within the Classroom

A quick verbal reminder is often used by teachers to remind a student of certain behavior expectations. Using nonverbal cues, such as the raising of the eyebrow, can also effectively remind a student that a classroom rule is being broken. Moving into a student's proximity and gently placing a hand on a shoulder may be the next logical step.

Chapter 2 discussed how the arrangement of furniture can affect behavior. Rearranging the seating plan can change the dynamics of classroom environment, isolate problem behaviors, and encourage positive interactions between different students.

Second Offense: Using the Space Outside the Classroom

Teachers should make it a priority to not participate in a disagreement with a student in front of the rest of the class. If a student is noncompliant, ask them to step outside for a moment. As soon as possible, step outside with the student to discuss the issue. Avoid keeping the student in the hall for long periods of time. It may take a minute or two before a natural break in the lesson occurs allowing you to step out. Keep the conversation to one minute. Ask the student to repeat the expectations for classroom behavior. Clarify the reason for the expectation and refer back to the classroom meeting where the rules and procedures for civility were discussed.

Third Offense: Teacher
Consequences and Parent Engagement

If the student demonstrates compliance, then use positive reinforcement on a regular basis to support the change in behavior. If the inappropriate behavior resurfaces from time to time, it may be necessary to go back to the strategies outlined in the first and second offense. If the behavior continues, a teacher-imposed consequence will be needed. At this point it's important for the teacher to get the message across to the student that they are in control and have the authority to exercise a consequence that will discourage the behavior. Often teachers will send the student to the office prematurely before following the next steps. When doing so, the teacher sends a message that they are not able to resolve issues that occur inside the classroom. Of course, certain behaviors, such as acts of violence, must be reported to the office immediately.

To initiate a consequence, ask the student to step outside the classroom. As in the previous situation, the time out of class should be brief, and the follow-up discussion outside the classroom should take no more than a minute. When speaking to the student, repeat the expectations and arrange a time to meet the student later that day, preferably at the end of class, at lunch, or after school depending on whether the student must catch a bus. Keep the meeting time brief—under five minutes. Use a private and nonthreatening space that isn't isolated from colleagues. This meeting is the first consequence. Longer detentions will penalize the teacher. If the detention is going to work, a brief one will accomplish the desired outcome. During the teacher-student conference, a further consequence may be assigned depending on the severity of the inappropriate behavior. Consequences may include an apology or volunteering. Inform the student that there will be a call home to share the issue and solicit parent support.

Fourth Offense: Engaging the Office

When a student continues to be noncompliant and the teacher has likely exhausted the resources available to change the behavior, the student may be sent to the office. The classroom strategies have not been working, and a new plan has to be developed.

Students should not be sent back to class during the period that they have been removed from class. Hopefully the teacher has already called home, and now it will be the administrator's decision to call the parents or guardians in to help resolve the problem.

Each school district will have a code of behavior that guides the decisions around appropriate consequences for certain behaviors (see Appendix F: Sample Code of Behavior). Administrators are responsible for following the code of conduct using a progressive discipline approach. When inappropriate behavior occurs, schools should utilize a range of interventions, supports, and consequences that are developmentally appropriate that include opportunities for students to focus on improving behavior. Consequences for inappropriate behavior may include but are not limited to the following:

- A meeting with the parent(s), student, and principal
- Referral to a community agency for anger management or substance abuse
- Detentions
- Loss of privileges
- Conflict mediation
- Peer mentoring
- Referral to counseling
- Reconciliation
- Restitution
- Suspension
- Expulsion

Maintaining Civility in the Classroom

The Progressive Discipline Model is supported by Maintaining Civility, outlined in Figure 4.5, which guides teachers during the progressive discipline process.

POSITIVE BEHAVIORAL INTERVENTIONS, SUPPORTS, AND CONSEQUENCES

The categorical rejection of disciplinary techniques is simply not supported by research. Quite the contrary, the research and theory strongly support a balanced approach that employs a variety of techniques.

—Robert Marzano (2003)

Let's examine the civil habit of punctuality and how taking responsibility for one's actions and being considerate of the needs of others becomes a demonstration of good character.

Figure 4.5   Maintaining Civility

Using Consequences in Maintaining Civility

We must instruct and lead not just the intellect of students but their moral and social processes as well.

—Dr. Philip Fitch Vincent (2005)

Model	It is still the best way to reinforce what the behavioral expectations are.
Be Visible	The best schools have staff members in their doorways before the start of each period.
Ignore Nothing	If inappropriate behavior is ignored, it sends the message to other students that it is okay.
Talk in Private	Use a kind voice. The student will always want to save face.
Contact Home	Parent support is critical.
Be Timely	Respond quickly and keep the conversation or consequence short.
Reinforce and Consequence	You have four options. They are to (1) do nothing, (2) be positive, (3) consequence, and (4) do both Options 2 and 3. Option 4 gets the best results. Option 1 gets no results.
Don't Kill a Fly With a Sledgehammer	Use the least amount of discipline to get the greatest result.
Make It Appropriate	If students are marking desks, have them wash desks. If students are wearing a hat, they lose the hat.
Make It Right	Restoration, reconciliation, or restitution. It's got to be one of those three.

Bottom Line—If you do not get results with a student, send the student to the main office.

Tick, Tock, Keep Your Eye on the Clock

Student lateness had been a problem at Huntsville high School for many years. It was deeply imbedded in the culture of the school. Over the years, both detention and suspension were used to deter students from being late to class. Success was limited.

In an attempt to move away from a punitive solution, the staff and administration collaborated in their efforts to change behavior. Through a series of staff meetings, with open discussion, the staff determined that lateness was the number one issue in the school. Over a six-week period data were collected on student lateness including times of day, locations, and number of students.

A promotional campaign was launched, which included posters, announcements, bulletin board displays, and changes to the physical environment, which included an increase in teacher visibility. The first step of the plan required the purchase of 100 new clocks, replacing every existing clock in the school. (These battery-operated satellite clocks have been a challenge in themselves.) The clocks were synchronized with the real-world time and the master clock in the main office. The breaks and use of bells were standardized to be consistent throughout the day. Each period ended with a bell followed by a five-minute warning bell. Each class started with a bell. Music was used in the morning and after lunch to signal that there were five minutes until classes were to start. The music ended one minute before the bell. The main foyer display case was set up with six clocks showing the time from each rural feeder area for Huntsville High—just like at the airport. Of course, all the clocks had the same time. Buttons were designed and worn by all staff showing a hairy eyeball inside a clock. The campaign was called *Tick, Tock, Keep Your Eye on the Clock.* It was fun, and it managed to create a school-wide dialogue around the importance of being on time. Classes that achieved perfect attendance on certain days were rewarded with treats. Students who were repeatedly late were assigned community service and given consequences if their behavior continued.

The plan worked for about six weeks. Lateness declined significantly over that period of time. However, as illustrated in Figure 2.1, Safe and Inviting Physical Environment, without a deeper change in the culture, the change was not likely to sustain itself—and it didn't.

Part 2 of the plan was called *Learn to Earn.* The promotion focused on the importance of being on time for work in order to keep a job and earn a living. Teachers were asked to monitor hallways on a voluntary basis. Students who were late for class were locked out until a teacher came around with a clipboard to record their name and then let them into class. Students arriving late to school required a late slip from the office. Data were kept on the prevalence of lateness and repeat offenders. The parents of repeat offenders were contacted and students did community service. Classes with perfect attendance were provided with lunch by the administration. The strategy was highly successful because a greater number of teachers became engaged in the process. The campaign was effective, rarely using suspension as a consequence. The Learn to Earn program is a good example of a schoolwide intervention that encourages students in this particular situation to be on time to class and stresses the importance of that behavior beyond school toward the world of work.

Huntsville High School provides many other interventions and supports to respond to difficulties that students are experiencing. The student services department works closely with outside agencies, such as Addiction Outreach and the District Health Unit, to set up counseling sessions for those students in need of support. They also offer a peer tutoring course. There is a growing commitment to service learning that teaches our students about the importance of being contributing citizens by valuing and serving others in need. The physical education department has joined with guidance to provide female students weekly support sessions to discuss issues that are important to them.

Consequences Versus Positive Reinforcement

Opposing viewpoints exist on the most effective way to maintain a civil environment. For example, many educators believe that punishment is not an effective method of changing behavior, and in some cases, it increases the undesired behavior (Stormont, Lewis, Beckner, & Johnson, 2008). The positive reinforcement approach emphasizes the introduction, modeling, and positive reinforcement of socially acceptable behavior.

The use of mild forms of punishment as a consequence can support a positive approach to teaching appropriate behavior (Marzano, 2003). Detention and reconciliation are examples of mild forms of punishment. Interestingly, calling home is ranked high by parents and students as a form of consequence—an action by the school personnel that is both negative and positive (Marzano, 2003).

There is a growing movement, based on research that supports the use of both positive interventions and supports, and consequences when educating students about appropriate behavior (Marzano, 2003). This approach, combining positive interventions and supports with clearly outlined consequences for inappropriate behavior, forms the framework for an effective approach to increasing positive behavior and teaching character traits such as respect and responsibility. Preventative strategies such as high expectations, early intervention and supports, and regular communication with parents can be used in conjunction with consequences to form an effective method of classroom management.

Though a punishment may be effective in reducing many behaviors, it is less likely to be effective with older children (Marzano, 2003), and the strategy may not promote positive relationships between staff and students. Compliance by certain students is achieved at the expense of building a positive working relationship between staff and students. This is one reason why developing good character is so difficult at the secondary school level. To develop a positive school climate, everyone in the building must be engaged and contributing to the progressive discipline model. That includes parents.

Schoolwide Systems of Discipline

Is there a connection between PBIS and character education? The answer is yes. The PBIS program focuses on developing a set of schoolwide, problem-solving strategies and processes for changing student behavior that are built on the strengths of the individual school. Character development focuses on the learning of attributes such as responsibility and respect that are also built on a foundation of common traits agreed upon by the school community. These two goals do go hand in hand.

Chapter 1 discussed the need to simplify a school's character development efforts by identifying real issues that relate to the climate of the school. Chapter 2 established the importance of creating a safe and inviting physical environment that nurtured positive behavior. The PBIS model promotes developing positive environments both inside the classroom and throughout all common areas of the school. Chapter 3 focused on staff modeling. The goal of the PBIS is to create a supportive environment through education, staff modeling, and the positive support of behavior that demonstrates good character. We can quickly see the strong connections between these two approaches to teaching appropriate behavior and developing good character.

According to the research studies sponsored by the PBIS group, one of the key components of a successful schoolwide discipline program is using a 4:1 ratio of positive reinforcement to consequences.

Several other strategies connect PBIS to the *Keep It Simple, Make It Real* approach to character development.

- Learning and teaching are valued.
- Aggressive and unsafe behavior is discouraged.
- Respect, responsibility, and cooperation are essential expectations for student behavior.
- Individual differences are valued.
- Priority is given to supporting individuals with special needs.
- Both approaches support an environment where opportunities for learning academics are enhanced.

Assessing the changes in the students' beliefs, attitudes, and behaviors in middle and secondary schools is a difficult task. Strategies for assessment will be discussed in Chapter 6. The comprehensive use of data collection by the PBIS program provides schools with a specific tool that can be used to monitor the effectiveness of character development strategies and programs. Collecting data around a specific behavior, such as swearing in the halls or lateness, can provide feedback on the effectiveness of the strategies used to teach character traits such as respect and responsibility. It may also eliminate the use of ineffective practices and initiate changes in the execution of the plan before time is wasted and the behavior deteriorates further.

The PBIS Triangle

One valuable tool created by the PBIS organization is the behavior triangle illustrated in Figure 4.6, Continuum of Schoolwide Instructional and Positive Behavior Supports.

The continuum shows where a typical population of students' behavior will be situated according to their need for positive support prevention. In a given population, 80% of the students will be compliant, regardless of the systems that are in place to educate, monitor, and respond to inappropriate behavior. Of the student population, 15% may identify with groups that require extra attention in the form of programs and responses to inappropriate behavior. These students are fence-sitters. They may be influenced to join the 80% or become the next group of at-risk students that form 5% of the population. Highly at-risk students require very specific intervention strategies to monitor and change inappropriate behavior. Marzano (1993) and Stormont, Lewis, Beckner, and Johnson (2008) agree that punishment is not likely to be effective with older, highly at-risk students.

The PBIS triangle provides an excellent model for analyzing trends in student behavior and developing a schoolwide behavior

Figure 4.6   Continuum of Schoolwide Instructional and Positive
Behavior Supports

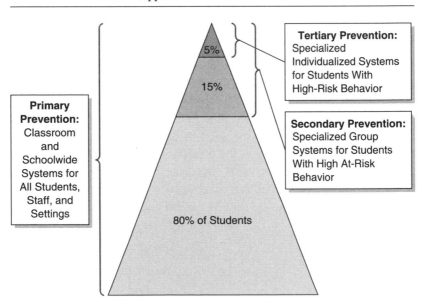

management plan that responds to specific issues within your school culture. Student behavior is a defining indicator of a student's acquisition of any one of the character traits that your character development program is trying to achieve.

For more information on PBIS, visit http://www.pbis.org.

Some Final Thoughts

The importance of creating a civil and orderly learning environment cannot be overstated. Establishing rules and procedures for civility guides students to learn the basic behaviors, such as respect for others, tolerance, compassion, and responsible citizenship, that typify good character. Deciding on what rules to enforce has never been an issue for educators. Developing procedures that students can use to practice the rules is a far greater challenge and where the real learning takes place.

There is a need for increased teacher training around creating what Dr. Philip Fitch Vincent (2005) describes as a caring, responsible, and productive school. Educating good character is not a quick fix operation. It requires expertise in developing strategies and procedures that form part of a schoolwide system for behavior management that meets the needs of each school culture. These systems will combine a little measure of old-fashion disciplining with a positive spin. There are no substitutes for traditional values such as consistency, timeliness, and fairness. However, our diversity requires us to take a deeper look at our school culture and the climate we teach in and where our students learn. Programs that provide intervention, support, democratic engagement, and positive reinforcement must be included as part of the progressive discipline plan for each school. Establishing a school climate where positive behaviors are valued will develop good character in students and enhance student academic achievement.

QUOTES

The presence of civility within our schools and communities may be a greater predictor of our successes in the next hundred years than our intellectual abilities.

—Philip Fitch Vincent (2005),
Restoring School Civility

Civil behavior defines a deeper sense of interrelationships, relationships built on a sense of benefit or benevolence toward others.

—David Wangaard (quoted in Vincent, 2005),
Restoring School Civility

Good manners are a stepping stone to being a remarkable human being.

—Robin Sharma (2006),
The Greatness Guide

CHAPTER FIVE

Making Curricular Connections

Teaching Opportunities That Connect Student Learning to Character Development

Where does character education fit into the curriculum? The simple answer is this: everywhere. Since education seeks to help students develop as a person, character development is part and parcel of the whole enterprise.

—K. Ryan and K. Bohlin (2003)

INTRODUCTION

The purpose of delivering a curriculum to students involves the dissemination of knowledge and the practice of skills that are connected to specific course contents in a particular field of study. In terms of delivering these curricula, teachers are well positioned to take up the challenge, given their high level of academic training, which is most often concentrated in specialized areas such as mathematics, science, language, and technology. However, if teachers aim to connect character development to teaching the academic curriculum, they must embrace a new definition and purpose for curriculum— one that will require a shift in thinking beyond traditional knowledge

97

and skills toward a much richer definition of what should be taught in schools.

The main purpose of this chapter is to provide a framework for shifting the way teachers think about the task of developing curriculum to a way that embeds character development into the instruction and becomes part of what students learn.

CURRICULUM PRIORITIES
IN CHARACTER DEVELOPMENT

Legislation

——————— ❦ ———————

Character development is not a new curriculum. Neither is it an add-on. It is embedded in all that we do in schools. It is intentionally infused in our policies, practices, programs, and interactions.

—Avis Glaze (2006)

Finding Common Ground, developed in 2006 by Avis Glaze at the Ontario Ministry of Education, is an example of a recent shift to embed character education into schoolwide curriculum. *The Heart of the Matter: Character and Citizenship Education in Alberta Schools* (Ministry of Education, 2005) provides the directive for that province. Both provinces have also passed Safe and Caring Schools legislation to support the development of respectful cultures, safe and secure learning environments, positive relationships, appropriate social behavior, and community involvement—all important components of a curriculum connected to character development. Ontario and Alberta are among other Canadian provinces that have introduced specific legislation that connects character education, equity and inclusion, and citizenship to the curriculum.

In the United States, Section 5431 of No Child Left Behind (NCLB) provides for the procuring of grants to support partnerships, curriculum research, and program development in character education. NCLB states the guidelines for measuring the integration of character education into the curriculum and the standards for success in fostering the identified attributes.

The expectation for teachers to actually integrate character education into their curriculum varies among school districts across North America. Over the past 10 years, state and provincial governments have recognized the importance of including character education in the culture and curriculum of the school. For example, the California Code of Education Section 233.5 (a) states the following.

> Each teacher shall endeavor to impress upon the minds of the pupils the principles of morality, truth, justice, patriotism, and a true comprehension of the rights, duties, and dignity of American citizenship, and the meaning of equality and human dignity, including the promotion of harmonious relations, kindness toward domestic pets and the humane treatment of living creatures, to teach them to avoid idleness, profanity, and falsehood, and to instruct them in manners and morals and the principles of a free government.

Section 233.5 (b) states that each teacher is also encouraged to create, and foster, an environment that encourages pupils to realize their full potential and that is free from discriminatory attitudes, practices, events, or activities, in order to prevent acts of hate violence.

California, Massachusetts, Florida, and 21 other U.S. states are participating in the Character Education Partnership's (CEP) State Schools of Character program, which requires a state to demonstrate the incorporation of the Eleven Principles of Character Education as outlined in the CEP's character development framework.

Teacher Training

Chapter 4 highlighted the lack of teacher university preparation in the area of classroom management. The same may be said for character development and a lack of training regarding connecting it to the curriculum. Compounding the issue, teachers spend their first years mastering course content. New teachers are often given multiple assignments and more challenging classes. Is there any question why teachers may feel that integrating character development is impossible to achieve? What goes on in the classroom, the place where changes are most difficult to implement, the place where character development is most difficult to achieve, is the topic of Chapter 5.

Connecting the curriculum to character development may be a question of priority. Teachers who demonstrate a clear intent to focus the curriculum on developing attributes in their students, such as critical-thinking abilities and problem-solving skills, resiliency, innovation, respectfulness, and confidence, embrace a much deeper teaching agenda.

The plan to integrate and infuse character education into the curriculum involves a few simple and real strategies that any teacher, new or experienced, can follow provided he or she is motivated to learn and apply them. Given that you are reading this book, you are likely well on the way to embracing new ways to connect the curriculum to your students.

Toward Embedding Character Development in the Curriculum

Figure 5.1, Curriculum Connections, shows the addition of the final foundation of the Character Development Framework for Schools.

The outer ring shows a few examples of curriculum activities that teachers can incorporate into their curriculum planning. Curriculum also includes the cocurriculum, meaning academic instruction embedded in activities beyond the walls of the classroom. These

Figure 5.1   Curriculum Connections

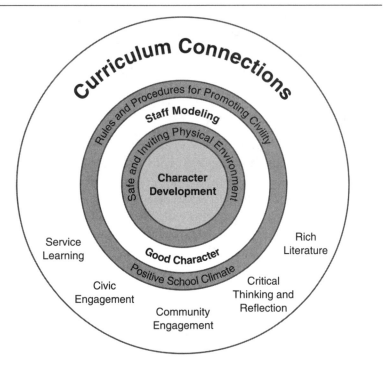

Source: Trillium Lakelands District School Board, Ontario, Canada. Reprinted with permission.

examples are not meant to be complete. In fact, the potential for relevant activities are limitless. The opportunities to connect the curriculum to character development are inspirited by the teacher's zest for innovation.

In *What Successful Principals Do,* Todd Whitaker (2003) draws the distinction between raising student achievement and the use of academic programs that are proven to bring about academic results. According to Whitaker, the use of successful academic programs does not always result in increased student success. His belief is that good people always come before good programs. His research supports the position that teachers who strive for excellence in themselves and their students by creating positive relationships, and aiming to foster good character by using the curriculum connections like those suggested in the Character Development Framework for Schools, create greater opportunities for student success. Whitaker says that a teacher's attitude toward his or her role in student learning, the motivation to change, and willingness to create a positive learning climate has the greatest impact on student achievement.

Performance and Moral Character

As you shift your focus to one of connecting character development to curriculum implementation, I suggest you make use of *Smart and Good High Schools: Integrating Excellence and Ethics for Success, Work, and Beyond* (Lickona & Davidson, 2005). This report shares the major findings from the study of 24 diverse and highly successful high schools

> Performance character is needed to realize our potential for excellence. Moral character enables us to treat others and ourselves with respect and care—and ensures that we use ethical means to achieve our performance goals.
>
> —Thomas Lickona
> and Matt Davidson (2005)

across the United States. The report outlines a whole-school approach to pursuing a mission of excellence and ethics.

The report defines character to include both performance and moral character. Performance character means striving for excellence and involves the development of character traits such as diligence, a strong work ethic, a positive attitude, and perseverance. Moral character consists of personal qualities such as integrity, caring, respect, responsibility, and cooperation. Students who develop good character demonstrate both performance and moral character (Lickona & Davidson, 2005).

When structuring your classroom or leading cocurricular activities, developing a classroom management plan or designing curriculum, you have an opportunity to connect performance and moral character.

Implicit and Explicit Approaches to Character Development: A Continuum of Strategies

—————— ✑ ——————

Treated separately, out of context, character education curriculum materials and programs are likely to have minimal effect on students.

—Edward DeRoche
and Mary Williams (2001b)

Chapter 1 touched on the various strategies that can be used to incorporate character education into a school, such as events, projects, programs, and models or frameworks. Though some educators may prefer one strategy over another, there is no one right way or one way that works better than another.

Chapter 5 focuses on identifying the essential components of the curriculum and modifying instruction to provide sufficient time to establish the relevance of the content to students' lives, more actively engage students in the learning process, and teach character development. The examples that follow include strategies that work in the classroom and beyond. Regardless of which strategies you or your school incorporates to teach character development, character can be taught both explicitly or implicitly, depending on the circumstances you find you and your student are in.

Figure 5.2, Implicit and Explicit Character Development Continuum, provides a perspective on various strategies that can be used to connect character development to the curriculum.

Thomas Lickona and Matt Davidson (2005) describe the three As of performance and moral character. They are awareness, attitude, and action. Aware students can identify and understand what is required to pursue excellence. Students who care about achieving excellence have a positive attitude and, as a result, are motivated and committed to doing the right thing in social situations. Students who take action have the skills and habits to take a stand and assume leadership for influencing others to do the right thing (Lickona & Davidson, 2005). From a simple and real perspective, connecting the curriculum to character

Figure 5.2   Implicit and Explicit Character Development Continuum

Implicit	Strategy	Descriptor
	Creating a safe and inviting physical environment	The design layout and appearance of the surrounding environment changes the way students think and behave.
	Staff modeling	A student's relationship with adults influences their behavior.
	Positive behavior interventions and supports	Appropriate student behavior increases as a result of positive reinforcement.
	Rich literature	Students study literary works with value-laden messages that stimulate critical thinking skills.
	Service learning	Students participate in community volunteerism and reflect upon the impact of their actions.
	Heroes	Students study the lives and actions of individuals that have demonstrated one or more character attributes.
Explicit	Mottos, credos, mission and vision statements, codes of conduct, athletic fair play policies, attribute of the month	Student behavior is guided by community-based virtues.

Continuum

development likely needs to achieve these three goals: (1) raising student awareness, (2) nurturing a positive attitude, and (3) developing the skills and habits required to take action.

THE RITE OF CURRICULUM PASSAGE

—————— ⚜ ——————

Educational change is technically simple and socially complex.

—Michael Fullan (2008)

A key focus of this chapter is to change your mindset toward curriculum development and instruction. If you begin each curriculum planning session by identifying the big ideas in the unit of study and then planning lessons, activities, assignments, and assessment that connect those big ideas with the character development of your students, then you will be more successful at developing students with good character as well as raising student achievement. Here I'm talking about how you structure your classroom and connect those big curriculum ideas to the teaching and learning of the performance and moral related attributes, such as being prepared and on time, respect, tolerance, compassion, and kindness.

The importance of reviewing your allocation of time, the relevancy of the curriculum, and the way your students are engaged are also important concepts in shifting the curriculum emphasis. The simple and real strategies outlined will demonstrate how to incorporate character development into lesson planning and cocurricular activities.

The Rite of Curriculum Passage defines an approach to delivering the curriculum that requires a pedagogical shift that will support the infusion and integration of character development into the curriculum.

Justin DeWeerdt

Justin DeWeerdt came to teach mathematics at Huntsville High School at the age of 31, after a short career as a civil engineer. Justin brought to his teaching a keen outlook that embraced innovation and forward thinking—something he had experienced in the competitive corporate world. Within one year of entering the profession, Justin became head of mathematics. Like his teaching, he brought an open mind to the possibility of leading change in his department.

One of the programs that Justin got involved in was Link Crew. Link Crew is a program that prepares elementary students for their transition to high school. It involves the training of senior high school students as Link Leaders. Students visit elementary feeder schools, as well as organize and deliver a high energy orientation one week before school starts. The program promotes safety, information, and connections.

Justin had the idea that it might be valuable to begin each semester of his mathematics classes with Link Crew activities. The purpose, like the orientation, would be to create a safe classroom space for students to learn, provide the information that students needed to be successful, and to build connections between everyone in the class. Justin's idea worked. The students were really excited about Justin's approach to learning, and they enjoyed coming to class. More important, the learning environment became a place where students felt they could share ideas and work through challenges.

Justin decided to make each lesson relevant to the lives of his students. Mathematics topics were selected that had an athletic or work related theme. Students were given the opportunity to self-select topics of interest that related to the curriculum.

To enhance the learning, Justin incorporated technology through the use of interactive whiteboards. Students learned how to use the technology by incorporating it into their own presentations to the class. Video technology was used to collect data and demonstrate physical relationships. Part of the activity required the students to become physically active in class, which increased student engagement in the lesson. Students often worked in groups to solve problems.

Incorporating these innovations into the lesson took time away from Justin's teacher-directed instruction and the students' seatwork. However, his students were highly engaged and more focused on the big ideas and concepts that supported the key learning outcomes from the curriculum. With this shift in emphasis, there were less behavior issues for Justin to deal with and cooperation, responsibility, and leadership were promoted.

A major professional development initiative by the Trillium Lakelands District School Board included an eight teacher-lesson study where teachers were excused from teaching for three days to develop one lesson that would promote positive student responses. Justin modeled the lesson for other teachers as they observed and took notes. Then the teachers met to reflect on the lesson. Justin also video-taped himself as a reflection tool for himself and his department.

Justin also started a mountain bike club. During his preparation period, and before his classes would begin, Justin would spend time in the hallways chatting with students and making sure that they were following the expectations for hallway behavior. He made a point of greeting his students at the classroom door. His connections outside the classroom equaled the success within the classroom.

Justin's approach to teaching demonstrates a clear example of how character education can be infused and integrated into the academic curriculum. The most significant outcome was an increase in student achievement. Justin's students achieved high test scores on the provincial Grade 9 math standardized test. And the efforts of each member of the mathematics department resulted in an increase of 16% on the provincial standardized math test.

Early in his teaching career, Justin made the transition, discovering the RITE of Curriculum Passage, focusing his professional development on the role that his teaching has on his students' achievement, as well as their character development. Let's look at the components required to make the transition.

> Students need to make connections with the content and learn about the connectedness between subjects.
>
> —Edward DeRoche (2004)

Figure 5.3, The RITE of Curriculum Passage, illustrates the factors that contribute to a curriculum focus that infuses character development as part of student learning.

The model in Figure 5.3 suggests a 20% reduction in curriculum. The percentage is intended to be neither prescriptive nor arbitrary but rather a reasonable guideline that teachers may follow to assist with the compacting of the curriculum. It is not uncommon to find teachers moving forward with the content despite the fact that a number of students are failing, or at least underachieving, not to mention having not taken the time to embed character development into their curriculum. Infusing character development into the curriculum is not intended to replace or add to existing curriculum. However, the recommendation is based on years of observation and repeated efforts to support secondary teachers as they push to get their students through an expanding curriculum.

The purpose of the reduction is to facilitate teaching in a way that is more relevant and focused on key ideas, more flexible with respect to time, and more engaging. Is the problem too much curriculum and not enough time? The problem of content overload requires teachers to constantly make choices regarding what content

Figure 5.3   The RITE of Curriculum Passage

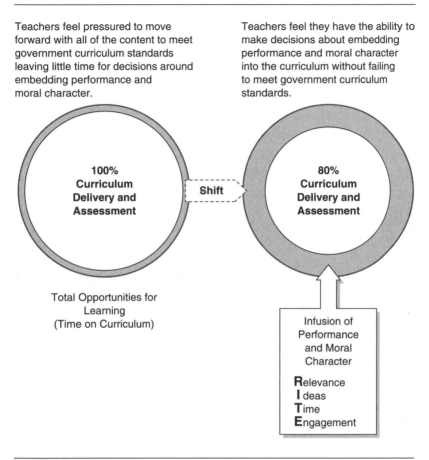

Teachers feel pressured to move forward with all of the content to meet government curriculum standards leaving little time for decisions around embedding performance and moral character.

Teachers feel they have the ability to make decisions about embedding performance and moral character into the curriculum without failing to meet government curriculum standards.

100%
Curriculum
Delivery and
Assessment

Shift

80%
Curriculum
Delivery and
Assessment

Total Opportunities for
Learning
(Time on Curriculum)

Infusion of
Performance
and Moral
Character

Relevance
Ideas
Time
Engagement

to emphasize, as well as what not to teach (Tomlinson & McTighe, 2006). If the goal is to infuse and integrate content that teaches character development, teachers must feel that they have the ability to make the choices that will incorporate character development into their classroom procedures and lesson plans. The key questions given these circumstances are listed below:

- Which essential big ideas and core processes should be incorporated into the curriculum to meet the content expectations and standards as set out by state or provincial guidelines—and which ones could be left out?
- Which character traits should the teacher infuse and integrate into the curriculum?

Once the essential outcomes are identified, character educators must focus their attention on the following four key instructional goals:

1. Finding *relevance* in the curriculum to the learner

2. Identifying the *big ideas* within the content

3. Providing extra *time* to allow critical thinking on issues connected to the big ideas

4. Increasing student *engagement* in the learning process

— ✺ —

A curriculum must be seen by students as relevant to their lives and aspirations.

—Thomas Lickona and
Matt Davidson (2005)

The teachers' next step is to identify which character traits they want their students to develop. Then using the four key instructional goals, weave the opportunities for character development into the class procedures and lesson plans.

Let's look at each area in more detail.

Relevance

The *R* in RITE stands for relevance. Learning is an active process related to one's personal experience (DeRoche & Williams, 2001b). Teachers who attend to their students' backgrounds and needs assist each student in making connections between themselves and the important content in the curriculum (Tomlinson & McTighe, 2006).

In *Character Education: A Primer for Teachers,* DeRoche and Williams (2001) recommend an instructional teaching framework called the Eight Cs. The Eight Cs guide teachers how to implement character education and describe teacher roles and responsibilities in the classroom. Here they are.

1. Connections: teacher modeling

2. Constructivism: a student-centered approach

3. Classroom Climate: creating a community of learners

4. Classroom Management: intrinsic motivation, rules, and rewards

5. Critical Thinking: ethical decision making and higher-order thinking and questioning

6. Conflict Resolution: mediation and problem-solving strategies

7. Cooperative Learning: the significance of interdependence

8. Community Service Learning: citizenship and democratic practices

The process starts by establishing strong teacher-student relationships. This will likely begin in the first few days of the year or semester by including students in a discussion about the decisions around classroom rules and what is needed to create a safe and caring classroom climate. Establishing expectations around task completion, lateness, readiness, and self-discipline develops a student's performance character needed to achieve excellence (Lickona & Davidson, 2005). Starting the class in this way also helps to establish the learners' conviction that they are valued by the teacher and becomes a potent invitation for them to take the risk implicit in the learning process (Tomlinson & McTighe, 2006).

Discovering the students' interest and connecting the lesson content to those interests is the next step in the process. Here are some teaching tips from DeRoche and Williams that will help to connect the curriculum to student interests:

- Encourage and accept student autonomy.
- Allow student responses to drive the lesson.
- Adjust content and teaching strategies to respond to students' needs.
- Inquire about student understanding.
- Encourage students to engage in dialogue.
- Encourage student inquiry by asking good questions and encouraging students to ask questions.
- Ask students to elaborate on their responses.
- Create a sense of mutual trust and respect in the classroom.
- Provide time for students to construct ideas and apply relationships.

Implementing these strategies helps to ensure that the curriculum is delivered in a way that is relevant to lives of the students and ensures that the students learn an ethical means to achieve their performance goals (Lickona & Davidson, 2005). Let's address the question of how to approach decisions around what must be taught.

Ideas

The *I* in RITE stands for ideas. *Understanding by Design* (UbD) (Tomlinson & McTighe, 2006) is a curriculum design model that demonstrates how and what to teach. It is a way of thinking that promotes the identification of big and essential endpoint content ideas, and the designing of curriculum backwards to create lessons that are meaningful to the students. Developing lessons that focus on these big ideas facilitates the teaching of processes and procedures that bring relevance to learning and enhance opportunities for teaching character education. An example of a big content idea that might be studied in a history or world issues course is the topic of genocide. Genocide may connect to the issue of bullying around the school and the importance of students developing tolerance for others.

The implementation of an UbD backwards design approach to planning the curriculum helps teachers to feel they have the ability to incorporate character education into the curriculum without failing to meet the expectations set forth by the government. UbD does this in a number of ways.

- It limits the curriculum to the essential components, thus leaving more time for students to develop a deeper understanding of the content.
- It reduces the time and effort required to develop, administer, and mark assessments that attempt to cover less essential components of the curriculum.
- It allows more time to engage the learners in critical thinking and problem solving around the deeper issues that connect to the curriculum and their lives.
- It allows for teacher flexibility in responding to student needs.

Identifying the big ideas when curriculum planning may relieve the pressures of making a choice about, who, where, how, and what to teach in order to integrate learning that relates to character development. Time is the next component of the RITE of Curriculum Passage.

Time

The *T* in RITE stands for time. Giving the gift of time to the process of teaching and learning may be the most valued decision a teacher can make. As mentioned previously, designing down and compacting the curriculum assist teachers with making decisions about which essential big ideas to include within the curriculum and how to embed the teaching of performance and moral related character.

I want to emphasize the importance of taking the time to teach the performance-related character traits, such as time management and task completion. For example, research shows that one of the factors that contributes to a lack of student achievement is assignment noncompletion leading to a mark of zero (Reeves, 2006). What a rich opportunity for you to work on performance character with students who have difficulty organizing and handing work in on time. Think of the strategies you could use to assist your student in improving time management and task completions, such as the following:

- Using an agenda
- Chunking the assignment into segments
- Submitting stages of work for formative feedback
- Allowing the opportunity to negotiate extensions
- Teaching ways to communicate problems and self-advocate for support

These are all simple ways to embed character development into your teaching without even needing to change what you teach.

Engagement

The *E* in RITE stands for engagement. Processes and procedures focus instruction on who is being taught. Designing the curriculum backwards around the big ideas provides more time and increases the teacher's flexibility to respond to student needs and uncover deeper issues connected to the curriculum that help students to examine their beliefs, attitudes, and behaviors. The final step in the RITE of Curriculum Passage is student engagement, which focuses on the big ideas by actively engaging the students in the learning process

Teacher must ask themselves two fundamental questions:

- How will I engage the learners?
- What are the values and ethical issues within the content that I teach and the activities, teams, events, and clubs that I supervise?

The answers to these two questions are needed to assist teachers in providing students with opportunities to examine their beliefs, attitudes, and behaviors and develop good character.

Let's take the example of a Grade 12 physical and health education exercise science course to work through answers to the questions above. One of the key themes in this program focuses on athletic injuries and rehabilitation. Students are asked to apply their knowledge of human anatomy and physiology to the identification and treatment of sport-related injuries. The teacher might assume that the students have successfully studied the body systems, parts, and functions, in order to move the discussion toward causes and treatments of specific body-area related injuries.

Scenario 1

In the first scenario, Teacher A wants to ensure that the students have an opportunity to study every major internal body system including the axial and appendicular skeletal systems that provide for stability and movement, to fully understand the extent of potential injuries that may result from overexertion.

The body is a complex system. Its comprehensive study requires the extensive memorization of strangely unfamiliar terms that identify parts of the anatomy and lengthy descriptions of functions and processes that make the body work. Teacher A knows this and develops a demanding curriculum designed to cover all of the systems and the injuries typically associated with each.

Most of the instruction is lecture style, supported by a few video clips, handouts with diagrams of the body, an article on sport injuries, and copious notes to be copied. There isn't enough time to cover it all in class, so Teacher A assigns memory work each night, followed by a quiz the next day.

Teacher A knows the curriculum, having studied kinesiology while attending university. While at school, the university professors expected students to memorize all of the key parts and functions of each body system in preparation for entering the workforce in a related field. However, the students in Teacher A's class are not going into a career related to physical education or sports medicine, with the exception of maybe one student.

At first, the students find the demands of learning new information interesting and challenging. But soon, combined with their other subject requirements, they quickly become worn down and disgruntled by the large volumes of information they must learn to successfully pass the course and receive the marks required to meet admission standards for postsecondary studies. In the end, a few students become experts in the field—others have become turned off and will never study sports injuries again.

Teacher A has not infused or integrated any character development into the lessons. Opportunities for critical thinking and the problem solving of issues related to sport injuries, which may foster a change in students' beliefs, attitudes, and behaviors, have been overlooked.

Scenario 2

Teacher B brings a different attitude to teaching exercise science. Recognizing that most of the students in the course will not move on to study sports medicine, Teacher B wants to ensure that the students receive a well rounded education that includes an appreciation for the complexity of the body and an understanding of the issues that may effect them in there own lives as they pursue recreational physical activities. Teacher B knows that many of the health-related decisions the students will make in the future are dependent on both knowledge of how the body works, as well as their beliefs, attitudes, and behaviors around healthy living.

Teacher B designs backward from these big ideas and decides to focus the unit lessons on two common injuries, ankle and knee sprains. Much like Teacher A, Teacher B uses materials such as videos and handouts to support the lectures on the knee and ankle. However, with the time that's available the students are given the opportunity to self-select a topic of interest for study that relates to their own life. One student chooses dance injuries, another running, and a third surfing.

The students are encouraged to identify sport-related issues that also have ethical implications. Examples of topics include alternative methods of injury treatment, the use of nutritional supplementation, and the availability of performance-enhancing drugs. Teacher B uses the study of these personalized topics as an opportunity to engage the students in discussions requiring critical thinking and problem solving. Ethics, integrity, and responsibility are all character traits that can factor into sport and sport injury management.

The students are excited about their assignments. Each lesson includes small-group discussions where students share their issues and problem-solve solutions. The learning environment is rich with opportunity to teach to the beliefs, attitudes, and behaviors of the students. Teacher B's approach may foster a change in students' beliefs, attitudes, and behaviors.

Teachers are under a lot of pressure to deliver 100% of the curriculum expectations. Principals can help teachers make the transition to a more student-centered classroom by providing professional development in UbD and differentiated instruction. Teachers need to be convinced that planning relevance, big ideas, time, and increased student engagement in the curriculum will improve the classroom climate, reduce classroom management issue, and provide opportunities to develop good character in students.

CURRICULAR AND COCURRICULAR OPPORTUNITIES THAT CONNECT STUDENT LEARNING TO CHARACTER DEVELOPMENT

—— ❧ ——

The basic premise of your selection of a character education curriculum is captured in the words "infusion" and "integration." Character education should not be considered an add-on. It needs to be a critical part of the existing school curricular and cocurricular programs. It needs to be integrated into the daily live of the classroom and the school.

—Edward DeRoche and Mary Williams (2001b)

To this point I have acknowledged most teachers' strong sense of duty and responsibility to deliver 100% of the course content and that it is one of the obstacles to successfully embedding character development into the curriculum. Establishing a curriculum that integrates moral character can be achieved when teachers identify the essential big ideas and then design instructional units backwards from those key components, thus reducing the need to cover all of the content. Opportunities for teaching performance character are provided through the structures and processes that you use to manage your class and the completion of school work.

Administrators can support teachers by encouraging them to use backward design in the students' best interest, both academically and developmentally. Principals can also help by ensuring that there are successful schoolwide strategies in place to respond to standardized testing. Achieving good scores on these tests takes the pressure off of administrators and staff to increasingly focus on that testing. As a result, more time can be spent doing what successful schools do (Whitaker, 2003), including the teaching of responsible citizenship, kindness, caring, perseverance, and tolerance for individual differences.

If you are looking for comprehensive outlines of lesson plans that demonstrate what and how to teach character development in their specific subject area, a few examples can be found in Resource A at the back of the book. That has not been my main purpose in writing this chapter. There are many high quality curriculum guides available for purchase that provide lesson plans on how to integrate character development into the curriculum. But here are a few interesting examples of how teachers have embedded character development into the curriculum. All of these units have required UbD planning. The examples are unique in that they were designed by the teachers to meet the needs of the students in that particular class while connecting the curriculum to the learning of character attributes. These locally developed interpretations of the curriculum demonstrate the innovative approaches of some of the teachers at Huntsville High School. Let's look at some of these examples.

Curricular

Arts

Huntsville High School has a vibrant visual arts department. Both the photography and media arts courses in that department have grown significantly. Students are highly engaged and keen to express themselves through their course work.

One of the essential learning outcomes of the Grade 12 media arts course is that students develop a *movie with a message*. The essential skills required to produce the movie are also an important part of student learning. The department organized a Films With Character festival. The students enrolled in the Grade 12 media arts course were responsible for a number of tasks including creating the movies, designing promotional materials, and assisting with event planning. Media arts students from the region's 10 high schools were invited to make submissions to the festival. Each film was judged by a professional panel.

The festival had a curricular focus. It also connected in a very significant way to two other larger initiatives. The festival was supported financially by Positive Behavior and Intervention Supports (PBIS) government funding. PBIS is an integral part of Huntsville High's positive behavior plan. The festival was also supported financially by our local district health unit. By engaging the community our students had the opportunity to work with the local health unit to promote messages about healthy living.

The festival was a huge success. During an afternoon performance, 400 elementary students from our feeder schools viewed the movies. An evening performance was organized for the community.

Numeracy

The Practical Academics and Life Skills (PALS) is a unique special education program at Huntsville High School. It is primarily a non–credit-generating program for developmentally challenged, high-needs students. The goal of the program is to teach these individuals the core life skills required for their successful integration into the community. One essential curriculum expectation is *money management.*

A service learning project that the PALS class undertook was called Coins for Chrysalis. Chrysalis is a nonprofit housing development in Huntsville that supports women in need of safe shelter. The service goal for the project was to collect money to support the shelter. PALS students collected jars of money from each homeroom. Their responsibilities included working in pairs to collect, count, and roll the money for banking. A mock store was set up in the PALS classroom so that the students could practice handling the money in various situations. Then students took the money to the bank to deposit and make a check for donation to Chrysalis. The project covered the expectations for numeracy skills and taught the students the importance of good citizenship.

Social Sciences

The curriculum guideline for the family studies department course *parenting and human development* examines *social structures and social challenges.* Students learn through practical experiences in the community factors that effect human development and impact on the quality of life.

The Grade 12 parenting class at Huntsville High School regularly visits Roger's Cove, a seniors' retirement community, to work with the residents. Students play card games, take seniors on walks, challenge them in computer games, and spend time listening to stories. The seniors appreciate the much needed companionship that comes from the students spending time with them. The students gain insights into human development during the later stages of life. The program is an excellent example of connecting community engagement to the curriculum.

Literacy

One of the optional Grade 12 English courses in the Ontario curriculum is university level, writer's craft. The course gives students an opportunity to improve their writing skills by developing analytical and creative modes of writing. Students also investigate opportunities for publication and writing careers.

One curriculum expectation is the *art and craft of writing.* Students must describe a new understanding of the writer's craft that they have acquired by attending a public reading of an author's work. Through independent study projects students are also expected to develop critical thinking skills around a controversial topic of interest, such as Aboriginal rights or the use of graffiti.

Slam Poetry is a challenging and creative form of literacy that involves writers performing their work in front of live audiences. Students act out their poetry using expressive language and body movements. It gives students an opportunity for self-expression on topics related to their lives.

At Huntsville High School, students presented their writing to class and then performed at the local community theatre along with visiting professional writers. After the performance, students attended workshops with the professionals. Developing critical thinking skills is an important part of becoming a contributing member of the community.

The *Slam Poetry* project was a great way to address the curriculum expectations of the course by incorporating a meaningful community event with topics that were relevant to the students' lives. The value of taking the time to organize and prepare for the performance was reflected in the students' high level of engagement.

Science and Technology

At Huntsville High School, each class was challenged to pay it forward by designing a small project to support the local community. Classes were given $150 of seed money to support their project. Some classes used the money to generate additional funding.

The Grade 11 college level biology course encourages hands-on exploration of real-world problems and issues that relate science to technology, society, and the environment. Specific curriculum expectations include the examination of *factors that influence the sustaining of the natural environment* and the *impact of human activity on the natural environment.* The biology class used its pay-it-forward money to rent a bus so that they could travel to a local provincial park for the day. The purpose of the trip was to work on building trails for the park users. The activity connected the students to the essential curriculum outcomes while providing a service to the provincial park users. The project afforded an excellent opportunity for the study of microbiology and plant structures—also part of the Grade 11 biology curriculum. The students had a great day.

Cocurricular

Civic Engagement

The Town of Huntsville Master Plan is developed through a series of community consultations where input is collected from citizens on the direction of future development. Town council has several goals in developing the plan. Encouraging local youth to stay at home, or return after postsecondary studies, is one of the main goals. Another goal includes the development of recreational facilities, particularly those connected to Huntsville's abundant natural environment. The plan is of particular interest to students.

A town hall was organized at the high school. Students from the senior politics class, athletic council, and student parliament were invited to prepare questions for the mayor and his counselors on topics of interest to the students. Students studied the key components of the Town of Huntsville Master Plan in advance so that meaningful questions could be directed to the mayor and his staff. It was an excellent opportunity for the students to become engaged in the local democratic process.

Equity and Inclusion

The Town of Huntsville is located approximately two hours north of Toronto. Though the residents are almost entirely white, issues of equity and inclusion still exist that are unique to the local region. The region has one of lowest socioeconomic standings in the province. The level of adult education is among the lowest in the province. The number of at-risk individuals is above the provincial average.

Two new programs have been developed at Huntsville High School that addresses these issues of equity and inclusion. Our breakfast program is a joint effort between the school parent council and teachers. Many of our students come to school on an empty stomach. Some go the whole day without eating. The program runs out of the hospitality kitchen using community, staff, and student volunteers. The service provides high-quality nutrition to as many as 145 students each morning. The goal is to provide a welcoming environment for those students to come into the school and prepare themselves for academic study.

The athletic program at the Huntsville High School is one of the best in the province. It tends to cater to the serious high-performance athlete. The addition of the Special Olympics program has been a great success. Athletes work side by side with our special needs students to teach them skills and nurture their love for physical activity and athletics. The PALS students participate in regional competitions and are recognized at the end-of-the-year athletic banquet. It's a great experience for everyone involved and raises our awareness of those that have different challenges.

SOME FINAL THOUGHTS

For some teachers, making the connections between the curriculum and character development is as simple as preparing a good spaghetti sauce. Throw a little of this and a little more of that and come up with an interesting mix of curriculum ideas that whets the palate of even the most resistant learner.

The reality is that for most teachers the task is far more complex. Competition for curriculum time is fierce, particularly in elementary and middle schools. It is becoming more so at the secondary level. Standardized testing tends to drive the instructional practices of teachers. A lack of teacher training in classroom management and character development exasperates the problem.

The RITE of Passage prescribes a different approach to instruction. It is based on the principles of UbD and differentiated instruction. It challenges teachers to form instruction around big ideas, leaving time and space for activities that are relevant to the students, thus increasing engagement.

Principals and teachers must open their schools and classrooms to collaboration through professional learning groups that support the shift required to successfully connect the curriculum expectations to character development. The simple and real approach to teaching character development, as part of each lesson, can become part of your teaching repertoire.

QUOTES

We must become active participants with the students in thinking, reading, and processing the curriculum.

—Philip Fitch Vincent (2005),
Restoring School Civility

A curriculum must, first of all, be seen by the students as relevant to their lives and aspirations, helping them to build a positive future.

—Thomas Lickona (1991),
Educating for Character: How our Schools can Teach Respect and Responsibility

When we seek to help each of our students come to an understanding of important yet abstract ideas and processes, we propose a shift in job description. Teaching for understanding calls for teachers to "uncover" the content.

—Carol Anne Tomlinson and
Jay McTighe (2006),
*Integrating Differentiated Instruction:
Understanding by Design*

CHAPTER SIX

Assessing Character Development

The focus once again is at the school site, where efforts to foster character education take place, where values are validated, where school personnel have a close relationship with students and their parents, where one needs to know what is working and what is not, and where character education will succeed or fail.

—Edward DeRoche and Mary Williams (2001b)

INTRODUCTION

Determining the extent to which a character education program has been successfully implemented is a complex task. Many existing assessment tools include the examination of all the potential variables that affect character development. Moral leadership, meaningful and challenging academic curriculum, parent and community engagement, and staff functioning are several of the key components of a successful program (Character Education Partnership, 2007).

Figure 6.1, Attributes, adds the ring of community and school-based attributes that your character development program strives to effect in all stakeholders.

Establishing community-based attributes is an important part of the character development process. This chapter, however, assumes that those attributes have been established and the focus of assessment is on school-level implementation.

Your school district may decide to assess the progress made in developing good character throughout the system, but likely on a school-by-school basis as defined by the target attributes. The Trillium Lakelands District School Board, in response to a Ministry directive, developed a system-wide assessment of school climate. Though the

Figure 6.1   Attributes

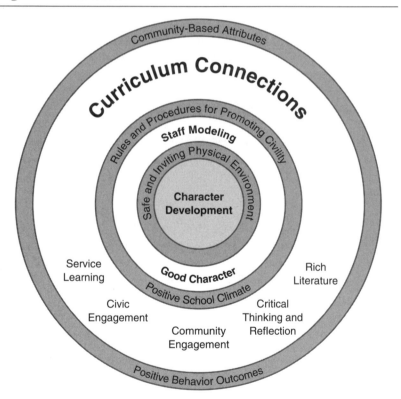

Source: Trillium Lakelands District School Board, Ontario, Canada. Reprinted with permission.

survey did not address the system attributes specifically, it did question how parents, staff, and students felt about the many aspects of school climate that are closely connected to character development. The survey results have been instrumental in the planning and implementation of strategies that respond to issues that affect a safe and caring school climate, such as bullying prevention and physical conditions of buildings.

The *Keep It Simple, Make It Real* approach to character development places a higher priority on what is happening inside the walls of a school. The underlying premise is that principals and teachers have more control, on a day-by-day basis, over what happens inside the school, than they do over what happens outside the school, within the community, and in the homes of their students. Efforts to engage families and community partners in the school's character education program are an important goal. However, it is more difficult to measure the changes in a families behavior or community actions than it is to measure the changes in student beliefs, attitudes, and behaviors.

This chapter focuses on monitoring students' behavior as part of an overall plan for developing good character, which includes the teaching of attributes such as responsibility and respect.

It is essential for schools to receive feedback on character education planning and implementation practices to ensure success. Monitoring of the program must be driven by results that can be measured. I don't recommend that a school attempt to focus on 10 attributes at one time. Selecting one or two attributes that are a priority for your school is the more effective strategy to follow.

What type of data need to be collected to assess a school's character development program? Let's begin with some key questions. What attributes has our school chosen to focus on? What behaviors are we observing throughout the school that demonstrates the learning of these attributes? How do the teachers, administration, and support staff respond to these behaviors? What variables need to be monitored to determine if student behaviors are changing? In what ways can teachers and principals share in the assessment process both inside and outside the classroom? Let's look at the guiding principles of monitoring and assessment as they apply to school improvement in general, followed by a few examples of assessments that work with the framework outlined in this book.

Monitoring Character Development

Clipboard

In Chapter 4, the concept of *establishing rules and procedures for civility* was introduced. Look back on page 90 and read the story Tick, Tock, Keep Your Eye on the Clock, which describes Huntsville High School's journey to develop performance character in students, specifically, getting to class on time.

In many ways, our original planning was excellent. The plan was simple—one goal. The plan was real—one targeted behavior that concerned staff more than any other. Staff wanted the students to take responsibility for being on time. The physical environment was taken into consideration—new clocks were purchased and appropriate signage was displayed. Staff modeled good character— by being at their own classroom on time. The rule was clearly defined—by developing procedures that helped students know what was expected. The Tick Tock plan had worked for periods of time but never sustaining itself beyond five or six weeks. We had difficulty understanding why our results could not be sustained.

After one and a half years of the Tick, Tock, Keep Your Eye on the Clock campaign, the clipboard was introduced. Classrooms were locked at the beginning of each class and students who were late were instructed to wait quietly outside their classroom until a teacher wrote down their name on a clipboard and unlocked the door to let them in.

Teachers voluntarily agreed to take five minutes at the beginning of their preparation period to monitor the halls, encourage students to get moving to class, record students who were late, and let them into their classroom. Teachers on similar preparation periods rotated the task.

This time the plan really worked. The successful execution of the plan lasted right up to the last day of the school year. Now teachers were out in the halls with clipboards in their hands. We asked ourselves in what way did that improve our chances for success? Here's the answer.

To be successful we needed to closely monitor the implementation of the plan. It began when teachers agreed to be more visible in the hallways and engage students around being on time. Teachers

> Schools are not helpless victims. Schools are integral in helping students form their character, make decisions, and acquire lifelong assets.
>
> —Douglas B. Reeves (2006)

also agreed to collect data and determine when students would be allowed to enter the classroom. Each week the data were collected and collated. Trends were established by analyzing the data. We started getting the answers to some of our key questions. Which students were repeatedly late? Which periods and times of day were students most often late? Which classrooms and areas of the school had the greatest number of lateness issues?

Students who were late three times were assigned a detention and their parents were contacted. Repeat offenders were withdrawn from class and assigned to an academic study resource room. If needed, parents were called in for interviews. The data collection also enabled us to track students who had experienced these consequences to see if their pattern of lateness was continuing. The data showed us that it was not.

For the first time in many years, staff agreed so strongly on the importance of changing the lateness problem that they were willing to become fully engaged in the solution. Administrators and teachers worked together to monitor the problem, and as a result, the students bought into the change. Students, who had previously indicated in our school climate survey that they knew the rules but they didn't feel that the teachers were enforcing them, were now seeing that everyone was committed to the change. The teachers' involvement in monitoring lateness demonstrated to the students that they were committed to changing behavior.

The Myths of Planning

A discussion on the topic of developing good character is also a discussion about school improvement. Douglas Reeves (2006) studied school improvement by examining what matters most in the way that schools approach positive change. His findings are presented in an insightful book titled *The Leading Learner.* Here is what he found out.

- Initiatives can be defined by three stages: (1) planning, (2) implementation, and (3) monitoring.
- Planning processes are less important than implementation, execution, and monitoring.
- Time, energy, and resources must be devoted to implementation, execution, and monitoring.

The three stages that guide schools from planning to performance are illustrated in Figure 6.2, Implementation Plan.

Douglas Reeves's research findings reveal that the majority of unsuccessful planning documents are devoted to compliance with format requirements established by outside forces, such as government. On the contrary, successful planning documents may be quite unique by design, and more important, the investment in time and resources is devoted to the execution of the plan.

So what does this mean for the character educator? How do Reeves's research findings guide the monitoring and assessment of a school's character development efforts? It may be best explained by Stephen Sample (2001), President of the University of Southern California, who believes that you can't copy your way to excellence. Original thinking and unconventional approaches are the keys to improvement. To connect Sample's idea to character development, let's revisit the first of the Principles of Action, introduced in Chapter 1, and build a case for *Keep It Simple, Make It Real* planning that can be easily implemented, monitored, and executed.

Figure 6.2   Implementation Plan

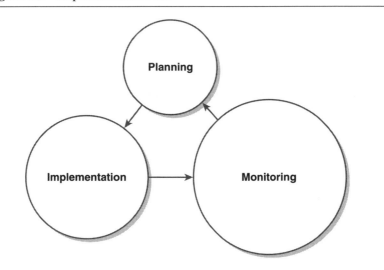

Monitoring—The Key to Successful Implementation

The first Principle of Action described in Chapter 1 is *motivation.* The vision for improving student beliefs, attitudes, and behaviors originates with one individual or a small group at best. However, the successful implementation of the character development plan relies heavily on the support of all of the school's stakeholders inside the school building. The research conducted by Positive Behavior Intervention and Supports strongly recommends that there must be an 80% buy-in required by staff before moving forward with the implementation of a behavior plan for students. Simply put, for any plan to be successfully implemented, the inner circle of staff supporters must grow to a sufficient size that a large number of teachers become willingly engaged in the execution of the plan—as finally became the case in the Tick, Tock plan at Huntsville High School. Conversely, the remainder of nonsupporters must be reduced to a small enough size so that, despite their best efforts to do so, they are unable to sabotage the implementation of the plan. Significant buy-in from staff during the implementation phase will result in staff support during the monitoring and data collection phase.

Because achieving 80% consensus is difficult at the best of times, it's important to focus on identifying only one goal for the character development plan—the one that everyone believes to be the biggest issue in the building. It's important to understand these concepts and believe in the importance of keeping the number of goals small and the issues really deep.

A good plan begins with a clearly communicated vision, usually defined by the principal. Typically, when the principal designs a plan for schoolwide character development, a small group of staff members will take part in the planning process. Often those individuals already buy-in to the proposed plan. That group forms the core of supporters that will attempt to sell the plan to the rest of the staff and drive the early stages of planning and implementation. This pattern of planning does not create a strong foundation for a successful character program.

If the successful execution of the plan is dependent on monitoring, then it will be important to widen the circle of support before moving into the implementation phase of the plan. The majority of staff must agree, prior to the implementation phase, that monitoring will be required. They must accept that monitoring is the only way to determine if the plan to develop student character is working. If the circle of influence is too small, then there will likely be resistance when monitoring is attempted and everyone's behavior is being examined.

An excellent way to achieve a strong foundation of support is to work outward from the principal and character development committee and begin to include department heads or division leaders in discussions regarding the behavior or attribute goal for the school. Getting input and finding out ways that each department can assist in the implementation and monitoring of the plan will be an important part of the success of the program. The last stage should include several staff meetings devoted to sharing and asking input on the character development plan and identifying how each staff member can take responsibility for the implementation and monitoring.

CREATING THE ASSESSMENT TOOL

—— ⚘ ——

You and the stakeholders at your school need to know the results of your efforts to develop children's character. The only way to do this is to appreciate the value in evaluation and then seek answers to the questions about the program and the anticipated outcomes.

—Edward DeRoche (2004)

After reading this chapter, you will, hopefully, be comfortable designing your own assessment tools that help evaluate the results of your efforts. Here are a few key guidelines that will help you develop your plan.

- Identify one or two goals for your character development program.
- Focus the planning on those goals and try to anticipate what the outcomes of the plan will be.
- Include discussions around the monitoring of outcomes of the plan before implementation begins.
- Allow at least two years for the successful implementation of the plan—one year to identify the goal and create the action plan and one year to implement the plan and monitor the results.
- Analyze the data two or three times a year during the implementation phase.

Key Questions

The first step of the assessment plan is the identification of key questions regarding what needs to be done and how your school is going to do it. For example, what behavior needs to be changed? What attribute do we want the students to learn? How does the school currently respond to inappropriate behavior? How can teachers and administration work together in a new way to educate students about appropriate behavior? What situations need to be monitored to determine if student behavior is changing and students have developed the attribute? Figure 6.3, Implementation Plan: Graffiti, is an example of a thumbnail implementation plan that identifies the appropriate questions for assessing the goal of reducing an aspect of vandalism.

In Figure 6.3, the goal is simple. A small group of individuals who are passionate about reducing graffiti have put together a three-step implementation plan that they think will increase student respect for the environment and ultimately lead to a reduction in graffiti. Before they begin to take action, by displaying student art work, increasing staff visibility, and introducing plants into the environment, they need to answer the key questions listed in the monitoring phase of the implementation plan. The answers to these, or similar key questions, will help guide the group toward the successful execution of the implementation plan.

Figure 6.3   Implementation Plan: Graffiti

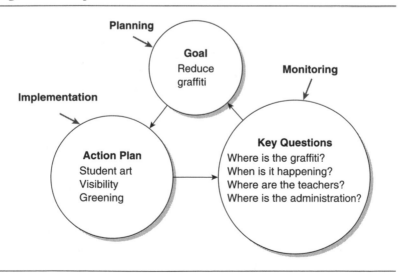

Data Collection

The group who is tackling the graffiti problem has identified key questions that need to be answered to assist them with their implementation and monitoring. They are now ready to move forward with the actual data collection.

Two key questions emerge regarding their next steps.

1. When do they begin collecting the data?

2. How do they get the data?

Let's look at the answers to these two questions.

When to Collect the Data

The time to plan for gathering data in a program evaluation is before the program itself begins (Bracey, 2006). Within that plan, provisions should be made to collect data before, during, and after the implementation of the plan. Why before? There are two main reasons.

First, it becomes extremely difficult to set targets for character development and measure changes in beliefs, attitudes, and behaviors if benchmarks have not been established prior to the implementation of the plan. You can't determine how far you have come if you don't know where you have come from. How will the graffiti group know if there has been a reduction in the behavior if they don't have some baseline data to compare to over time? How will they know if students' attitudes have changed regarding their respect for property?

The second reason relates to the implementation of the action plan. How will the group know where to put the resources, time, and energy if they don't know in advance all of the variables that could affect the success of the plan? In Figure 6.3, the group identified three action items: (1) student art, (2) visibility, and (3) greening. How will the group know where to put the student art, increase the visibility, and add the plant and flower arrangements if they don't know where the graffiti is taking place? It may also be important to anticipate which group of students hang out in that area, have an interest in art, and would be willing to join the group. The same could be said for the teachers and their willingness to supervise certain areas of the school.

Anticipate the variables that may affect the execution of the plan by determining exactly what the plan is supposed to do (Bracey, 2006). Anticipating the variables that affect student beliefs, attitudes, and behaviors will form an essential part of the assessment process prior to implementation.

Collecting data during the implementation phase provides feedback on the success of everyone's efforts during the early stages of implementation. In Chapter 1, Principle 4: The Dip, describes the typical situation when, in the early stages of the program, students appear to demonstrate changes in their attitudes and behavior. Then somewhere around the fifth or sixth week students begins to revert back to their original behavior. That's an excellent time to collect some progress data to determine what is working and what part of the plan needs some fine-tuning.

Collecting data toward the end of the year provides feedback on how well the plan was executed. Avoid collecting any data during the last couple of weeks of school. Everyone is getting tired. Allow enough time to summarize the findings and begin the process of revising the next stage of the plan to be implemented in the new school year.

How to Get the Data

Most educators do not have the time or expertise to concern themselves with the reliability, validity, correlation coefficiency, and statistical significance of the data being collected. Rather, educators often rely on compelling personal experience and example to draw conclusions about why something is happening and what needs to be done to change it (Bracey, 2006). The exception may be when assessing the academic progress of a student, in which case the teacher uses test results to evaluate performance and then report the findings using a grading system that relates in some way to the data. Even here, the teacher is well advised not to make important decisions about individuals or groups on the basis of a single test (Bracey, 2006). That is why teachers use a variety of assessment tools, such as tests, portfolios, and self- and peer-assessments to determine the progress of a student. The same principles apply when assessing the progress of your character development program.

In *The Action Research Guidebook*, Richard Sagor (2005) discusses the research challenge of educators working in a data-rich environment where life exists and data are continually being created by what people choose to do and what they elect not to do. Attempts to understand the particular circumstances, norms of behavior, and meanings attached to the behavior by the students in a specific school or classroom can potentially occupy a lot of time and energy.

The following section of this chapter describes how educators can approach the assessment of character development programs. The creation of the assessment tool is based on Sagor's (2005) guidelines. Sagor suggests using a *triangulated data-collection plan,* which uses three independent sources of data, to filter what is being collected and increase the credibility of the conclusions. For example, the graffiti group needs to select three independent sources of data to determine the best starting point for their plan. They may choose to gather insights from their colleagues through interviews, keep daily records of the number and specific locations of graffiti throughout the school, or photograph areas of the building where graffiti is prevalent. The group may also choose to record students' perceptions of their environment. An examination of teacher supervision schedules may provide some insight into visibility patterns by staff.

The sources of data used by the graffiti group may have some relevance during the implementation phase. For example, has the amount and location of graffiti changed in any way? Have students perceptions of their environment changed as a result of the improvements made by including student art and more plants in certain areas of the school?

Tables 6.1, 6.2, and 6.3, Assessment Tool: Graffiti, provide a thumbnail data collection tool that the graffiti group could use prior to implementing their action plan. The purpose of these tools is to assist the group in determining if what they anticipate might work as a plan is likely to create the desired outcomes.

The purpose of Table 6.1 is to collect data regarding the frequency and location of the graffiti.

A decision must be made regarding who will collect the data. It may be an administrator, committee members, or individual staff members. As more individuals become engaged in the process, the buy-in and willingness to share the responsibility will be greater. Here are a few suggestions when staff can increase involvement:

- Teachers: at the end of each period, in their area of instruction
- Department or division heads: at the end of each period, in their department areas
- Custodial staff: in their cleaning area at the shift change
- Character education committee members: at the end or beginning of each day
- Administration: at any point in time while walking the building

Table 6.1   Assessment Tool: Graffiti

Pre-Implementation Planning Phase **Target Behavior: Graffiti** **Frequency and Location of Graffiti** **Data Collection Period 6 to 12 Weeks** **Week of** _____					
Location (i.e., floor, department, classroom, stairwell)	**Description** **(i.e., size, color, type of marker, unique styling)**				
	Monday	*Tuesday*	*Wednesday*	*Thursday*	*Friday*

Table 6.2 collects data on the perceptions of staff. Their experiences will vary from individual to individual. Some staff may not have noticed the graffiti at all. That may indicate something to the group about that individual's level of awareness of the issue or visibility around the building. Staff perceptions are important. This assessment will tell the graffiti group how teachers view the issue, which may be very helpful in determining what steps are needed to increase buy-in.

A reasonable cross-section of teachers, educational assistants, and support staff are required to get valid sampling of opinions and feeling on the issue. Having each group or committee member interview one person may be an effective way to survey the staff. Interviews need not be more than fifteen minutes in length.

Table 6.2   Assessment Tool: Graffiti

Pre-Implementation Planning Phase
Target Behavior: Graffiti
Staff Perception of Graffiti
Reflective Interviews
Interview Questions
Please comment on the following and rate your support for each statement.
The school is graffiti free.   (Low) **1 2 3 4 5 6 7 8 9 10   (High)**
Locations?
Times?
Frequency?
Other?

Staff are concerned.   (Low) 1 2 3 4 5 6 7 8 9 10 (High)

Colleagues discuss?

Staff report?

Removed immediately?

Other?

School climate/culture is positive.   (Low) 1 2 3 4 5 6 7 8 9 10   (High)

Physical setting is inviting?

Students care about the building?

Students interact with adults?

Other?

Table 6.3 asks the students how they feel about their safety at school, how students treat the building, and their perceptions about the role that staff take in caring for the physical environment. The survey attempts to anticipate and get information about the variables that may affect the implementation of the plan.

All three parts of the assessment tool are designed by the group, based on the questions they have about what may be happening in the building that might explain why students vandalize their school with graffiti. I recommend reading Edward DeRoche's (2004) *Evaluating Character Development* to explore great ideas on measuring your character development successes. Resource B provides other examples of assessment tools that fit with each ring of the Character Development Framework for Schools.

The theme of *Keep It Simple, Make It Real: Character Development in Grades 6–12* is based on the Six Principles of Action outlined in Chapter 1. This book has emphasized action—in particular, Principle 6, doing versus thinking. Creating a safe and inviting physical environment, staff modeling good character, establishing rules and procedures for civility, and making curriculum connections are all calls to action. I hope this book has provided an opportunity for learning. I encourage you to commit to focusing on the character development in your school—and then take action!

SOME FINAL THOUGHTS

Time and motivation are key factors when conducting action research. Keep it simple, make it real. Focus on one issue at a time. Move slowly through the process. Allow up to two years to widen the circle of buy-in by building a core group of leaders and then working the issues through with the staff at single-agenda staff meetings.

A common mistake that administrators and teachers make is that they don't come to terms with what it is that they need to work on together to develop positive beliefs, attitudes, and behaviors in students. Educators fail to recognize the powerful influence they can have on the character development of their students, as well as the climate of the school by changing just one behavior, such as graffiti.

Table 6.3   Assessment Tool: Graffiti (Student Perception of Graffiti
Secondary Survey)

Student Perception of Graffiti

Secondary Survey

Please do not put your name on the paper.

Name of your school: _____ What grade are you in? _____

Think about each sentence. Check the box that best fits what you think about your school.

		Strongly Agree	Agree	Disagree	Strongly Disagree
1.	This is a good school.				
2.	Students at this school are well behaved.				
3.	I understand how the school staff expects me to behave.				
4.	I feel safe everywhere in this school.				
5.	There is a staff member at school I can talk to if I have a problem.				
6.	I feel safe on the way to and from school.				
7.	Adults at this school care about the students.				
8.	Students do not bully each other at this school.				
9.	My teachers maintain an organized and clean physical space for me to work.				
10.	I treat the school building with respect.				
11.	I know of students who graffiti the school.				
12.	Teachers are visible throughout the building.				
13.	Adults at school expect me to treat the school with respect.				
14.	My school is well maintained and is in good condition.				
15.	The adults at school always know what's really going on.				

It's important to not just pay lip service to the problem. Persevering with the planning and implementation through monitoring and making adjustments will eventually result in the successful execution of the plan. Once the staff sees results, more individuals will buy in and the potential for tackling other issues successfully will increase.

QUOTES

Personal experiences are compelling, and in many situations, we must rely on them because we have nothing else.

—Gerald W. Bracey (2006),
Reading Educational Research

The acts of teaching and learning present problems that are among the most complex endeavors any professional ever has to deal with. And the front-line workers in education, the teachers and administrators working in schools, are the only people in a position to design adequate solutions to these challenges.

—Richard Sagor (2005),
*The Action Research Guidebook:
A Four-Step Process for Educators and School Teams*

Resource A

*Sample Character Development
Framework for Schools:
Trillium Lakelands District School Board*

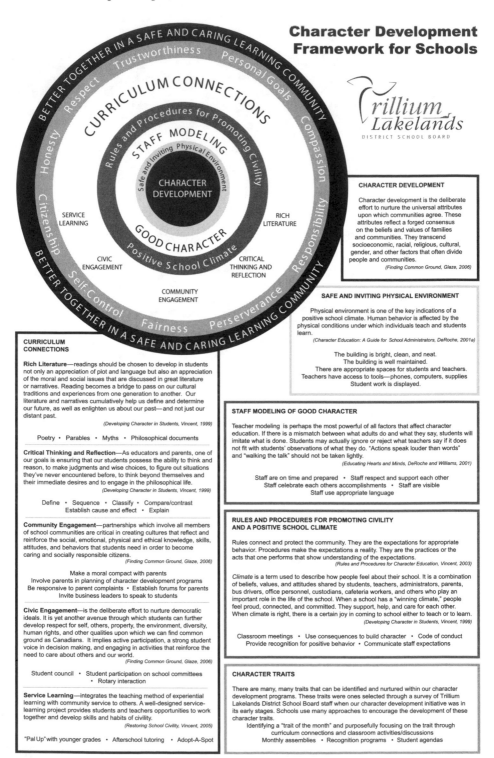

Character Development Framework for Schools

Trillium Lakelands DISTRICT SCHOOL BOARD

BETTER TOGETHER IN A SAFE AND CARING LEARNING COMMUNITY

Trustworthiness · Respect · Honesty · Citizenship · Self Control · Fairness · Perseverance · Responsibility · Compassion · Personal Goals

CURRICULUM CONNECTIONS

Rules and Procedures for Promoting Civility

STAFF MODELING

Safe and Inviting Physical Environment

CHARACTER DEVELOPMENT

GOOD CHARACTER

Positive School Climate

SERVICE LEARNING · CIVIC ENGAGEMENT · COMMUNITY ENGAGEMENT · CRITICAL THINKING AND REFLECTION · RICH LITERATURE

BETTER TOGETHER IN A SAFE AND CARING LEARNING COMMUNITY

CHARACTER DEVELOPMENT

Character development is the deliberate effort to nurture the universal attributes upon which communities agree. These attributes reflect a forged consensus on the beliefs and values of families and communities. They transcend socioeconomic, racial, religious, cultural, gender, and other factors that often divide people and communities.
(Finding Common Ground, Glaze, 2006)

SAFE AND INVITING PHYSICAL ENVIRONMENT

Physical environment is one of the key indications of a positive school climate. Human behavior is affected by the physical conditions under which individuals teach and students learn.
(Character Education: A Guide for School Administrators, DeRoche, 2001a)

The building is bright, clean, and neat.
The building is well maintained.
There are appropriate spaces for students and teachers.
Teachers have access to tools—phones, computers, supplies
Student work is displayed.

STAFF MODELING OF GOOD CHARACTER

Teacher modeling is perhaps the most powerful of all factors that affect character education. If there is a mismatch between what adults do and what they say, students will imitate what is done. Students may actually ignore or reject what teachers say if it does not fit with students' observations of what they do. "Actions speak louder than words" and "walking the talk" should not be taken lightly.
(Educating Hearts and Minds, DeRoche and Williams, 2001)

Staff are on time and prepared · Staff respect and support each other
Staff celebrate each others accomplishments · Staff are visible
Staff use appropriate language

RULES AND PROCEDURES FOR PROMOTING CIVILITY AND A POSITIVE SCHOOL CLIMATE

Rules connect and protect the community. They are the expectations for appropriate behavior. Procedures make the expectations a reality. They are the practices or the acts that one performs that show understanding of the expectations.
(Rules and Procedures for Character Education, Vincent, 2003)

Climate is a term used to describe how people feel about their school. It is a combination of beliefs, values, and attitudes shared by students, teachers, administrators, parents, bus drivers, office personnel, custodians, cafeteria workers, and others who play an important role in the life of the school. When a school has a "winning climate," people feel proud, connected, and committed. They support, help, and care for each other. When climate is right, there is a certain joy in coming to school either to teach or to learn.
(Developing Character in Students, Vincent, 1999)

Classroom meetings · Use consequences to build character · Code of conduct
Provide recognition for positive behavior · Communicate staff expectations

CHARACTER TRAITS

There are many, many traits that can be identified and nurtured within our character development programs. These traits were ones selected through a survey of Trillium Lakelands District School Board staff when our character development initiative was in its early stages. Schools use many approaches to encourage the development of these character traits.
Identifying a "trait of the month" and purposefully focusing on the trait through curriculum connections and classroom activities/discussions
Monthly assemblies · Recognition programs · Student agendas

CURRICULUM CONNECTIONS

Rich Literature—readings should be chosen to develop in students not only an appreciation of plot and language but also an appreciation of the moral and social issues that are discussed in great literature or narratives. Reading becomes a bridge to pass on our cultural traditions and experiences from one generation to another. Our literature and narratives cumulatively help us define and determine our future, as well as enlighten us about our past—and not just our distant past.
(Developing Character in Students, Vincent, 1999)

Poetry · Parables · Myths · Philosophical documents

Critical Thinking and Reflection—As educators and parents, one of our goals is ensuring that our students possess the ability to think and reason, to make judgments and wise choices, to figure out situations they've never encountered before, to think beyond themselves and their immediate desires and to engage in the philosophical life.
(Developing Character in Students, Vincent, 1999)

Define · Sequence · Classify · Compare/contrast
Establish cause and effect · Explain

Community Engagement—partnerships which involve all members of school communities are critical in creating cultures that reflect and reinforce the social, emotional, physical and ethical knowledge, skills, attitudes, and behaviors that students need in order to become caring and socially responsible citizens.
(Finding Common Ground, Glaze, 2006)

Make a moral compact with parents
Involve parents in planning of character development programs
Be responsive to parent complaints · Establish forums for parents
Invite business leaders to speak to students

Civic Engagement—is the deliberate effort to nurture democratic ideals. It is yet another avenue through which students can further develop respect for self, others, property, the environment, diversity, human rights, and other qualities upon which we can find common ground as Canadians. It implies active participation, a strong student voice in decision making, and engaging in activities that reinforce the need to care about others and our world.
(Finding Common Ground, Glaze, 2006)

Student council · Student participation on school committees
· Rotary interaction

Service Learning—integrates the teaching method of experiential learning with community service to others. A well-designed service-learning project provides students and teachers opportunities to work together and develop skills and habits of civility.
(Restoring School Civility, Vincent, 2005)

"Pal Up" with younger grades · Afterschool tutoring · Adopt-A-Spot

Resource B

Sample Assessment and
Evaluation Tools for the Character
Development Framework for Schools

Curriculum Connections

Teachers aiming to connect character development to the curriculum must embrace a new definition and purpose for curriculum—one that requires a shift in thinking beyond traditional knowledge and skills toward a much richer definition of what should be taught in schools. This assessment tool is intended for teachers—to assist them in measuring their use of the RITE of Passage and what impact their teaching has had on their students' learning experience.

Directions

Which of the following strategies have you incorporated into your instruction in the past three months? Please check off each one used.

Relevance

One of the critical roles for which teachers assume responsibility is determining the backgrounds, interests, and motivations of each student in their classroom. Teachers who attend to their students' backgrounds and needs assist each student in making connections between themselves and the important content in the curriculum.

- ❏ Encourage and accept student autonomy
- ❏ Allow student responses to drive the lesson
- ❏ Adjust content and teaching strategies to respond to my students' needs

- ❐ Inquire about my students' understanding
- ❐ Encourage students to engage in dialogue
- ❐ Encourage student inquiry by asking good questions and encouraging students to ask questions
- ❐ Ask students to elaborate on their responses
- ❐ Create a sense of mutual trust and respect in the classroom
- ❐ Provide time for students to construct ideas and apply relationships

Ideas

Developing lessons that focus on big ideas facilitates the teaching of processes and procedures that bring relevance to learning and enhance opportunities for teaching character education.

- ❐ Limit the curriculum to the essential components leaving more time for students to develop a deeper understanding of the content
- ❐ Reduce the time and effort required to develop, administer, and mark assessments
- ❐ Allow more time to engage my students in critical thinking and problem solving around the deeper issues that connect to the curriculum and their lives
- ❐ Allow for flexibility in responding to my student needs

Time

- ❐ Allow the time needed to get to know the students and focus on the big content ideas to create opportunities for increased student engagement

Engagement

- ❐ I have created lessons that hook in and engage my students.
- ❐ I have identified and included the values and ethical issues in the content that I teach and the activities, teams, events, and clubs I supervise.

Rules and Procedures for Civility

Respondent

- ❐ Teacher
- ❐ Student
- ❐ School Support Staff
- ❐ Administrator
- ❐ Parent
- ❐ Male
- ❐ Female

Directions

Using the scale below, circle the number that best represents your opinions about the extent to which these inappropriate behaviors occur in the common areas of the school.

4 = great extent   3 = some extent

2 = very little   1 = not at all

Behaviors	In the Common Areas				In the Classroom			
Bullying	4	3	2	1	4	3	2	1
Fighting	4	3	2	1	4	3	2	1
Swearing	4	3	2	1	4	3	2	1
Vandalism	4	3	2	1	4	3	2	1
Teasing	4	3	2	1	4	3	2	1
Name calling	4	3	2	1	4	3	2	1
Taunting	4	3	2	1	4	3	2	1
Ridiculing	4	3	2	1	4	3	2	1
Blaming	4	3	2	1	4	3	2	1
Stealing	4	3	2	1	4	3	2	1
Substance abuse	4	3	2	1	4	3	2	1
Threatening	4	3	2	1	4	3	2	1
Other	4	3	2	1	4	3	2	1

Specify _____

Safe and Inviting Physical Environment

The *Keep It Simple, Make It Real* approach to character development encourages educators to address the most basic needs of students first—those being physiological, health, and then safety. The individual growth and character development of adolescents are dependent on these foundations being met. There is a significant relationship between controlling the physical environment and student achievement and behavior. The purpose of this tool is to assess your willingness to make changes to the physical teaching environment.

Directions

Please answer the following questions as best as you can. The questions focus on the impact that your teaching has had on the students' physical environment.

A. The Physical Environment Can Be Controlled

How have you changed the physical environment in your classroom (i.e., seating arrangement, use of plants)?

_____

_____

B. The Physical Environment Can Affect Student Behavior

What changes have you noticed in your students' behavior (i.e., respect for others, movement around the class, willingness to get involved, and more focused activity)?

_____

_____

C. The Physical Environment Can Improve Academic Achievement

What changes in academic performance on assessments and standardized tests for reading, listening, languages, and arithmetic have you observed since changing the physical environment?

_____

_____

D. The Physical Environment Can Affect the Way Teachers Teach

How have you changed your approach to teaching (i.e., more enthusiastic, briskly paced lessons, effective questioning)?

_____

_____

E. The Physical Environment Changes According to the Needs of the Curriculum

How have you changed the configuration of your classroom to facilitate the use of computers, interactive whiteboards, the Internet, media arts, and other various technologies?

_____

_____

Staff Modeling Good Character

Your ability to teach, and your willingness to reflect on your practice, will have a significant impact on the quality of interactions with the students in your classes. This tool focuses on the skills that teachers use to develop increased self-awareness and the awareness of others. The assessment tool is designed as a self-reflection tool for teachers. It can also be used effectively in small professional learning groups, divisional teams, or departments to guide discussion around modeling good character.

Directions

Using the response key below, please circle your opinion on each of the following statements.

5 = strongly agree	4 = agree	3 = no opinion
2 = disagree	1 = strongly disagree	

Modeling the Inner Work

Meditation: I take short pauses to breathe   5   4   3   2   1
during the work day to help get in touch
with my physiology, emotions, and
attitudes at the moment.

Prayer: I take a few moments throughout   5   4   3   2   1
each day to sit in a state of reflection and
connect with my higher spirit, request
guidance, and give thanks for what I have.

Journaling: I have a personal journal that   5   4   3   2   1
I use to deposit ideas, theories, and random
thoughts, and I make journaling part of
a regular activity that my students
and I engage in together.

Reflective Reading: I read for short periods of   5   4   3   2   1
time each day to nurture my personal growth.

Spiritual Friendship: I have one colleague   5   4   3   2   1
I can trust to listen, know my darkest fears,
to push me when I need encouragement, and
comfort me when I'm feeling overextended.

Modeling Courageous Conversations

Listening: When someone is speaking   5   4   3   2   1
to me, I stop and suspend all other
activity.

Being Empathetic: I take the position   5   4   3   2   1
that each student concern I receive is very
real to them.

Trusting: I share authority by delegating   5   4   3   2   1
responsibility and work collaboratively
with my students.

Being Respectful: I know how to listen   5   4   3   2   1
without being judgmental or defensive.

Risk Taking: I willingly share ideas in a   5   4   3   2   1
freethinking atmosphere. The idea of
freethinking suggests participating in
dialogue without the fear of ridicule or
taking matters personally.

Resource C

Sample Strategic Plan for Schoolwide Character Development

Character Development Framework

Model Component	Description/Definition	School Targets (selected from system attributes)
Character Development	Character development is the deliberate effort to nurture the universal attributes upon which communities agree. These attributes reflect a forged consensus on the beliefs and values of families and communities. They transcend socioeconomic, racial, religious, cultural, gender, and other factors that often divide people and communities.	• Goal 1: Responsibility (being on time for class) • Goal 2: Respect for Property (reduction of graffiti) • Goal 3: Tolerance for Individual Differences (prevention of bullying)

Safe and Inviting Physical Environment	Physical environment is one of the key indications of a positive school climate. Human behavior is affected by the physical conditions under which individuals teach and students learn. For example, the building is bright, clean, and neat. The building is well maintained. There are appropriate spaces for students to learn and teachers to teach.	• Goal 1: Responsibility (lateness)
		Action Plan
		  ○ Clocks are located in key areas of building and classrooms
		  ○ Bells are used consistently
		  ○ Music is used to cue the students
		  ○ Posters are used to promote appropriate behavior

(Continued)

Model Component	Description/Definition	School Targets (selected from system attributes)

	Teachers have access to the tools they need—phones, computers, supplies. Student work is displayed.	• Goal 2: Respect for Property (graffiti)
		
		Action Plan
		
		  o Administration is visible
		  o Custodians monitor the building regularly
		  o Graffiti is removed immediately
		  o Student art work is posted
		  o Walls are clean and freshly painted
		  o Plants are used
		  o Furniture is provided for students
		
		• Goal 3: Tolerance for Individual Differences (bullying)
		
		Action Plan
		
		  o Posters created by students promote tolerance
		  o Quotes painted at entranceways
		  o Day of Segregation creates physical experience for students

Staff Modeling Good Character	Teacher modeling is the most powerful of all factors that affect character education. If there is a mismatch between what adults do and what they say, students will imitate what is done. Students may actually ignore or reject what teachers say if it does not fit with students' observations of what they do.	• Goal 1: Responsibility (lateness)
		
		Action Plan
		
		  o Staff arrive on time to work
		  o Staff are at their classroom before the students
		  o Staff greet students at the door as they arrive
		  o Staff report lateness diligently

Model Component	Description/Definition	School Targets (selected from system attributes)
	Actions speak louder than words. For example, the staff is on time and prepared. They respect and support each other, celebrate each others' accomplishments, are visible, and use appropriate language.	○ Staff call home and provide appropriate counseling ○ Staff provide consequences where necessary • Goal 2 Respect for Property (graffiti) *Action Plan* ○ Classrooms are clean and organized ○ Markings on desks are removed immediately ○ Maintenance staff make minor repairs to furniture and equipment in a timely fashion ○ Teachers display student work ○ Bulletin boards are relevant and kept up to date ○ Teacher keeps desk and teaching materials orderly • Goal 3: Tolerance for Individual Differences (bullying) *Action Plan* ○ Teachers demonstrate kindness and caring when dealing with inappropriate behavior ○ Teachers show an interest in all students ○ Teachers share and celebrate cultural differences in the classroom ○ Staff work cooperatively with other staff by sharing resources and team teaching

(Continued)

(Continued)

Model Component	Description/Definition	School Targets (selected from system attributes)

Rules and Procedures for Promoting Civility	Rules connect and protect the community. They are the expectations for appropriate behavior. Procedures make the expectations a reality. They are the practices or the acts that one performs that show understanding of the expectations.	• Goal 1: Responsibility (lateness)
		
		Action Plan
		  ○ Students must be on time to class (rule)
		  ○ Students must be moving in the halls after the 5 minute warning bell
		  ○ Music stops 60 seconds before students must be in class
		  ○ Students who are late are recorded
		  ○ Students must present to their teacher a late slip from the office if the reason for lateness is acceptable (procedure)
		  ○ Teachers reward students who are on time with time off or alternative activities
		  ○ Teachers recognize student responsibility with good news calls home
		  ○ Teachers present recognition certificates to students

Positive School Climate	*Climate* is a term used to describe how people feel about their school. It is a combination of beliefs, values, and attitudes shared by students, teachers, administrators, parents, bus drivers, office personnel,	• Goal 2: Respect for Property (graffiti) *Action Plan* ○ No marking of lockers or walls without permission from administration (rule)

Model Component	Description/Definition	School Targets (selected from system attributes)
	custodians, cafeteria workers, and others who play an important role in the life of the school. When a school has a "winning climate" people feel proud, connected, and committed. They support, help, and care for each other. When climate is right, there is a certain joy in coming to school, either to teach or to learn. For example, schools develop a code of conduct, use classroom meetings to build democracy, and provide positive reinforcement for appropriate behavior.	o Students are given opportunities to design and display student messages or art work in specific areas of the school o Students discuss the importance of showing respect for individual and the property of others during classroom meetings (procedure) • Goal 3: Tolerance for Individual Differences (bullying) *Action Plan* o Students will show tolerance for each individual's uniqueness as a person (rule) o Students will not block hallways o Students will speak respectfully to other students o Students will take a leadership role by mentoring younger students (procedure)
Curriculum Connections	Community engagement establishes partnerships, which involve all members of school communities that create a culture that reflects and reinforces the social, emotional, physical, and ethical knowledge, skills, attitudes, and behaviors that students need to become caring and socially responsible citizens.	• Goal 1: Responsibility (lateness) *Action Plan* o Students, parents, teachers, administration, and community organizations work together to create a breakfast program for students, which encourages disadvantaged students to come into the school and get to class on time

(Continued)

(Continued)

Model Component	Description/Definition	School Targets (selected from system attributes)
	Service learning integrates the teaching method of experiential learning with community service to others. A well-designed service-learning project (i.e., "pal up" with younger grades, after school tutoring, and adopt-a-spot) provides students and teachers opportunities to work together and develop skills and habits of civility.	• Goal 2: Respect for Property (graffiti) *Action Plan* o Students undertake a project to build a school in an underdeveloped country
	Rich literature provides readings (i.e., the use of poetry, parables, myths, and philosophical documents) chosen to develop in students an appreciation of plot and language, as well as moral and social issues that are discussed in great literature or narratives. Reading becomes a bridge to pass on our cultural traditions and experiences from one generation to another. Our literature and narratives cumulatively help us define and determine our future, as well as enlighten us about our past—and not just our distant past.	• Goal 3: Tolerance for Individual Differences (bullying) *Action Plan* o Students study great stories about the Holocaust such as *The Diary of Anne Frank* and *Unlocking the Doors: A Woman's Struggle Against Intolerance*

Resource D

Sample Lesson Plans

Sample Lesson Plan: History
Curricular Connections to Character Development

Potential Connections to Character Attributes

- Tolerance for diversity
- Citizenship
- Responsibility
- Respect for others
- Compassion
- Fairness

Relevance

- Students are given an opportunity to select topics of interest related to human rights that are relevant to issues in their lives.
- Students share their views and work on problem solving together to develop a deeper understanding of critical issues related to human rights, genocide, politics, economics, government, and religion.
- Students develop citizenship by exploring ways to become empowered to deal with local issues.

Big Ideas

- How does history teach us lessons about virtues such as tolerance and citizenship? Students explore big ideas associated with human rights and making personal choices (i.e., Who am I and how can I contribute to making my community, country, and the world a better place to live? What information do I need to make smart choices regarding lifestyle and good citizenship?).

Time

- Students have the time to focus on personal interests while meeting the standards and expectations for the course.

Engagement

- Students develop responsibility by engaging in the content that relates to their life, their families history, and the future of their country.
- Students have the opportunity to examine their own and others beliefs, attitudes, and behaviors regarding racism, genocide, and actions that violate human rights.
- Students examine the moral and ethical issues that affect their lives and the lives of others.
- Students are active in the learning process by working individually, in small groups, and as a whole class.

Sample Lesson Plan: History

Subject: History

Grade Level: Grade 10

Core Unit: Communities: Local, National, Global	**Topic: National** Identity
Lesson(s): Holocaust	**Lesson Length: 4–5**

Curriculum Standard

- Students will explore local, national, and global forces that shape national identity since WWI.
- Students will investigate the challenges presented by economic, social, and technological change and explore the contributions that individuals and groups made to culture and society during this period.
- Students will use critical thinking and communication skills to evaluate various interpretations of the issues and events of the period.

Students will

- explain the impact of the experience and memory of the Holocaust,
- explain human rights legislation,
- understand the nature of response to occurrences of genocide and ethnic cleansing, and
- evaluate how selected international political trends or events have a contribution to national decisions to engage in international activity (i.e., using nuclear weapons).

Learning Strategies	
Content Instruction (according to student interest) *i.e., explain, model, demonstrate, rehearsal, elaboration, organization, conceptualization, skill development*	**Student Activities (suggested)** *i.e., whole-class, pairs, individuals, small groups based on readiness, learning profile, interests)*
• Analyze significant events related to the Holocaust (e.g., the rise of anti-Semitism and Nazism; Kristallnacht; establishment of ghettos, concentration camps, and death camps) • Describe atrocities committed during World War II and assess the government's response to them • Describe Human Rights legislation • Research examples of genocide and ethic cleansing • Compare and contrast past and present government responses • Examine society's moral obligation to respond proactively to these examples	• Reading *Anne Frank* or *Unlocking the Doors: A Woman's Struggle Against Intolerance* • Discussing the injustices of the Holocaust and how it relates to current situations of inequity in the world • Working in small groups to create a photo petition using photography and art • Speaking on local radio to raise awareness of local and global issues related to equity • Web-based researching to determine government contacts and addresses • Writing letters to the newspaper media and government encouraging them to take action against countries that violate human rights

Sample Lesson Plan: Senior Physical Education
Curricular Connections to Character Development

Potential Connections to Character Attributes

- Personal goals
- Self-control
- Responsibility
- Respect for one's self
- Integrity

Relevance

- Students are given an opportunity to select topics of interest related to personal health and fitness that are relevant to issues in their lives.
- Students share their views and work on problem solving together to develop a deeper understanding of critical health issues related to the health business, the influence of the media, fitness research, and government.
- Students developed personalized strategies to improve their own health and fitness.

Big Ideas

- Students explore big ideas associated with health and performance-related fitness that lead to personal choices (i.e., who am I and what types of fitness goals make sense for my lifestyle, motivation, and interests? What are the benefits to sport-specific training? What type of information do I need as a consumer to make smart choices regarding the selection of health programs and products?).

Time

- Students have the time to focus on personal interests while meeting the standards and expectations for the course.

Engagement

- Students are hooked into the content because it relates to their life.

- Students have the opportunity to examine their own and others beliefs, attitudes, and behaviors.
- Students examine the moral and ethical issues that affect their lives.
- Students are active in the learning process by working individually, in small groups, and as a whole class.

Sample Lesson Plan: Senior Physical Education

Subject: Physical and Health Education

Grade Level: Grade 12

Core Unit: Personal   **Topic: Body**
Fitness Training   **Weight Management**

Lesson(s): Dieting and Supplementation
Lesson Length: 4–5 Lessons

Curriculum Standard

- Students will demonstrate knowledge of physiological and sociological concepts, principles, and strategies that apply to the learning and performance of physical activities.

Students will

- obtain knowledge of guiding principles for healthy weight reduction and maintenance,
- analyze commercial diet programs according to approved healthy guidelines,
- understand the metabolic effects of commercial dietary supplements on human metabolism, and
- critically analyze the regulatory guidelines for the health supplement industry.

Learning Strategies	
Content Instruction (according to student interest) *For example, explain, model, demonstrate, rehearsal, elaboration, organization, conceptualization, skill development*	**Student Activities (suggested)** *For example, whole-class, pairs, individuals, small groups based on readiness, learning profile, interests*
• Define terms (i.e., performance versus health related fitness) • Understand concepts of weight loss and gain • Examine literature on weight reduction guidelines • Compare and contrast diet programs • List ingredients and properties in diet supplements • Research diet program and supplement regulations • Discuss prevalent issues related to obesity, weight loss, etc. • Discuss the role of media and business in promoting health and fitness products and trends • Make personal health program decisions	• Teacher-directed guidelines/regulations lecture • Jigsaw study of diet programs • Individual research on contents of one supplement—small group presentations • Class debate or forum on newspaper article or published research relating to current social health issue—may be specific to a sport • Develop a informative brochure on topic of interest (i.e., use of certain type of supplement) • Write letters to government regarding regulation of sales of diet supplements • Develop a marketing plan for a specific program or product • Create a personalized weight reduction, gain, or maintenance plan

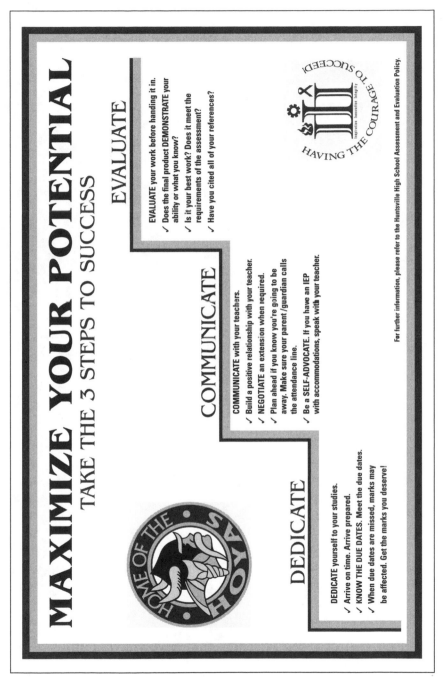

Resource F

Sample Code of Behavior

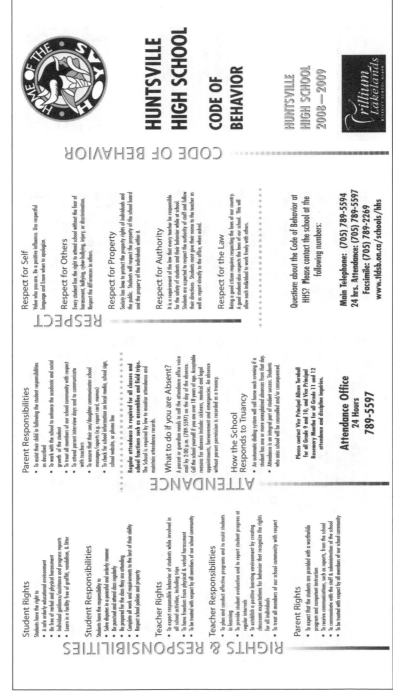

HUNTSVILLE HIGH SCHOOL

CODE OF BEHAVIOR

HUNTSVILLE HIGH SCHOOL 2008—2009

Trillium Lakelands DISTRICT SCHOOL BOARD

CODE OF BEHAVIOR

RESPECT

Respect for Self
Value who you are. Be a positive influence. Use respectful language and know when to apologize.

Respect for Others
Every student has the right to attend school without the fear of harassment, bullying, cyber-bullying, injury, or discrimination. Respect the differences in others.

Respect for Property
Society has laws to protect the property rights of individuals and the public. Students will respect the property of this school board and the property of the individuals within it.

Respect for Authority
It is a requirement of the law that every teacher be responsible for the safety of students and their behavior while at school. Students are expected to respect the authority of staff and follow their directions. Students must give their name to the teacher as well as report directly to the office, when asked.

Respect for the Law
Being a good citizen requires respecting the laws of our country. A good student also respects the laws of our school. This will allow each individual to work freely with others.

Questions about the Code of Behavior at HHS? Please contact the school at the following numbers:

Main Telephone: (705) 789-5594
24 hrs. Attendance: (705) 789-5597
Facsimile: (705) 789-2269
www.tldsb.on.ca/schools/hhs

ATTENDANCE

Parent Responsibilities
- To assist their child in following the student responsibilities as described
- To work with the school to enhance the academic and social growth of the student
- To treat all members of our school community with respect with teachers
- To attend parent interview days and to communicate with teachers
- To ensure that their son/daughter communicates school messages/reports (e.g. report card, memos)
- To check for school information on local media, school sign, school website, or phone line

Regular attendance is required for all classes and school functions such as assemblies and field trips. The School is required by law to monitor attendance and maintain attendance records.

What to do if you are Absent?
A parent or guardian needs to call the attendance office voice mail by 2:00 a.m. (789-5597) on the day of the absence. Call the school yourself if you are over 18 years of age. Acceptable reasons for absence include: sickness, medical and legal appointments, bereavement and emergencies. An absence without parent permission is recorded as a truancy.

How the School Responds to Truancy
- An automatic dialing system will call home each evening if a student has one or more unexplained absences from that day.
- Attendance is an integral part of student success. Students who miss school will be counselled and/or consequenced.

Please contact Vice Principal Alison Turnbull for all Grade 9 and 10, and Vice Principal Rosemary Manitou for all Grade 11 and 12 attendance and discipline inquiries.

Attendance Office
24 Hours
789-5597

RIGHTS & RESPONSIBILITIES

Student Rights
Students have the right to:
- A safe, orderly educational environment
- Be free of verbal and physical harassment
- Individual guidance/assistance and progress reports
- Learn in a facility free of graffiti, vandalism, & litter

Student Responsibilities
Students have the responsibility to:
- Solve disputes in a peaceful and orderly manner
- Be punctual and attend class regularly
- Be prepared for the class they are attending
- Complete all work and requirements to the best of their ability
- Respect school policies and property

Teacher Rights
- To expect responsible behavior of students while involved in all school activities, including trips
- To have freedom from physical & verbal harassment
- To be treated with respect by all members of our school community

Teacher Responsibilities
- To plan and conduct effective programs and to assist students in learning
- To provide student evaluation and to report student progress at regular intervals
- To establish a positive learning environment by creating classroom expectations for behavior that recognize the rights for all individuals
- To treat all members of our school community with respect

Parent Rights
- To expect that the students are provided with a worthwhile program and competent instruction
- To receive communications, such as reports, from the school
- To communicate with the staff & administration of the school
- To be treated with respect by all members of our school community

CODE OF BEHAVIOR

Student Dress Code
Students are expected to be neat and clean. Clothing must not display anything offensive to others. Hats, bandannas, and hoods are not allowed in school unless approved by the administration.

Hallways
Students are allowed in the hallways during the middle 20 minutes of each class, during lunch, between classes, and before and after school. Please use the benches for sitting and the garbage cans for garbage.

Announcements
Students are expected to stop what they are doing and be quiet during announcements.

School Property
Students should demonstrate respect for school property. Any damages will be assessed and appropriate consequences determined. Note: Lockers are the property of HHS. Please, no graffiti or vandalism.

Displays of Affection
HHS is a hand-holding school only.

Smoking
Tobacco products are not to be displayed or used anywhere on school property.

Buses
Students must follow the bus regulations as posted at the front of the bus. Obey the instructions of the bus driver. It is a privilege, not a right for students to ride a bus.

Visitors
Visitors must sign in at the office.

Computer Use
Students must comply with the school computer use policy.

Plagiarism
Information that you use in a school project that comes from any source (book, newspaper, Internet) other than your personal experience must be properly acknowledged. Failure to do so is called plagiarism and is considered a serious matter resulting in a mark of "0".

Use of Technology
- Cell phones (with or without camera capabilities) and personal handheld devices are to be turned off and be out of sight between 8:00am and 3:40pm. They may be used responsibly in the cafeteria.
- Use of the camera capabilities of electronic devices is forbidden in areas where there is an expectation of privacy (i.e., washrooms, change rooms).
- Students are personally responsible for their own devices and any activity and content on those devices or the Internet accessed by their passwords.

- Students are accountable for off-school property behavior using Internet sites or electronic devices which has a negative impact on the school environment and are subject to disciplinary measures for such behavior.

The above includes the use of the Internet or other technologies to threaten, harass, or demean another member of this school community, especially when those actions interfere with that member's safety or ability to function in the school.

Unacceptable Behavior: defined as verbal, physical, or electronic device/Internet actions intended to inflict physical, or psychological harm on targeted person(s). Examples:
- Harassment, including sexual harassment
- Bullying
- Intimidation or discrimination based on

- Racial background
- Ethno cultural background
- Religion
- Linguistic differences
- Sexual orientation
- Disability
- Class/income level or occupation
- Any other intolerance

Any unacceptable behavior, targeting any member of the school community, will be interpreted as impacting on the moral tone of the school.

The Trillium Lakelands Board Policy on Code of Conduct clearly specifies potential consequences for certain behaviors.

Suspension
A Principal may suspend a pupil for a fixed period of 1–20 days from his or her school, and from engaging in all school-related activities, if the pupil commits any of the following infractions while at school or engaged in a school-related activity:
- Uttering a threat to inflict serious bodily harm on another person
- Possessing alcohol or illegal drugs
- Being under the influence of alcohol or illegal drugs
- Swearing at a teacher or at another person in a position of authority
- Committing an act of vandalism that causes extensive damage to school property at the pupil's school or to property located on the premises of pupil's school
- Bullying

Expulsion
The following behaviors may lead to suspension and possible expulsion of 21 days or greater:
- Possessing a weapon, including possessing a firearm
- Using a weapon to cause or to threaten bodily harm to another person
- Committing physical assault on another person that causes bodily harm requiring treatment by a medical practitioner
- Committing sexual assault
- Trafficking in weapons or illegal drugs
- Committing robbery
- Giving alcohol to a minor
- Bullying

PROGRESSIVE DISCIPLINE

Huntsville High School has developed a progressive discipline model to determine the appropriate response to unacceptable behavior. In each instance, the administration will consider a student's individual circumstances, the nature and severity of the behavior, and the impact on the school climate.

Counseling
With peer, parent, teacher, department head, vice principal and/or principal, and may be formal or informal depending on the circumstances. The purpose may be to enlighten, educate, or warn the individual involved.

Temporary Removal From Class
Students will be removed from class and will be assigned academic support for one or more periods.

Detention
Students may be required to serve a detention or lunchtime duty.

Alternative Programming
Parents, staff, student, and administration will explore alternative programming.

Restorative Justice
Students may perform work, pay costs for damages, or make an apology.

Removal From Course
The student will be removed from a subject for part or all of the semester and will be provided with a supervised academic work period.

Temporary Loss of Privileges
Will involve temporary loss of services provided by the board of education. This may include bus riding privileges, computer use, and extracurricular activities.

Police Involvement
Appropriate charges may be laid.

Suspension
Will result in removal of the student from the school property and the loss of bus riding privileges. The student may be in the custody of the parent or guardian for up to 20 days.

Expulsion From School
May be recommended to the board of education by the principal, when a student's behavior is so unacceptable that his or her presence is injurious to other pupils. Such action will result in a hearing conducted by the board.

References

Balscovich, J., & Tomaka, J. (1991). Measures of self-esteem. In J. Robinson, P. Shaver, & L. Wrightsman (Eds.), *Measures of personality and social psychological attitudes* (pp. 115–160). San Diego, CA: Academic Press.

Bender, P. U. (1997). *Leadership from within.* Toronto, Ontario, Canada: Stoddart.

Benninga, J. S., Berkowitz, M. W., Kuehn, P., & Smith, K. (2003). The relationship of character education implementation and academic achievement in elementary schools. *Journal of Research in Character Education, 1*(1), 19–23.

Blase, J., & Blase, J. (1994). *Empowering teachers: What successful principals do.* Thousand Oaks, CA: Corwin.

Blase, J., & Kirby, P. (1992). *Bringing out the best in teachers: What effective principals do.* Thousand Oaks, CA: Corwin.

Bosworth, K. (1995). Caring for others and being cared for: Students talk caring in schools. *Phi Delta Kappan, 76*(9), 686–693.

Bosworth, K., & Ferreira, M. (2000). Context as critical factors in young adolescents' concept of caring. *Journal of Research in Childhood Education, 15*(1), 117–128.

Bowers, J. H., & Burkett, C. W. (1989). Effects of physical and school environment on students and faculty. *The Educational Facility Planner, 26*(1), 28–29.

Bracey, G. W. (2006). *Reading educational research.* Portsmouth, NH: Heinemann.

Building minds, minding buildings: Turning crumbling schools into environments for learning. (2006). Washington, DC: American Federation of Teachers.

California Code of Education. Section 233.5. (1999). *Character Education.* Sacramento, CA: California Department of Education.

Character education by design: A blueprint for successful district and school initiatives. (2007). Baltimore: Maryland Department of Education.

Covey, S. (2004). *The seven habits of highly effective people.* New York: Simon & Schuster.

Dean, S., Leithwood, K., & Leonard, L. (2004). *Creating safe and caring communities in Canada: Together we light the way.* Ottawa: Government of Canada.

DeRoche, E. (2004). *Evaluating character development: 51 tools for measuring success.* Chapel Hill, NC: Character Development Group.

DeRoche, E., & Williams, M. (1998). *Educating hearts and minds: A comprehensive character education framework.* Thousand Oaks, CA: Corwin.

DeRoche, E. & Williams, M. (2001a). *Character Education: A guide for school administrators.* Scarecrow Press, Lanham, MD.

DeRoche, E., & Williams, M. (2001b). *Character education: A primer for teachers.* Allen, TX: Argus Communications.

Earthman, G. I. (2002, October). *School facility conditions and academic achievement.* Blacksburg: Virginia Polytechnic Institute.

Earthman, G. (2004, January 5). *Prioritization of 31 criteria for school building adequacy.* Blacksburg: Virginia Polytechnic Institute and State University.

Eleven Principles of Effective Character Education. (2007). Washington, DC: Character Education Partnership.

Evans, R. (2008). *Trillium Lakelands District School Board School climate survey.* Unpublished manuscript.

Florence, M., Asbridge, M., & Veugelers, P. J. (2008). Diet quality and academic performance. *Journal of School Health, 7*(4), 209–215.

Fullan, M. (2008). *The six secrets of change: What the best leaders do to help their organizations survive and thrive.* New York: Jossey-Bass.

Gardner, H. (1999). *The disciplined mind: Beyond facts and standardized test: The K–12 education that every child deserves.* New York: Simon & Schuster.

Glaze, A. (2006, October). *Finding common ground: Character development in Ontario schools, K–12.* Toronto, Ontario, Canada: Ministry of Education.

Godin, S. (2007). *The dip.* New York: Penguin Group.

Helm, C. (2007, January/February). Teacher disposition affecting self-esteem and student performance. *Clearing House: A Journal of Educational Issues and Ideas, 80*(3), 109–110.

Holfve-Sabel, M. A. (2006, March). Comparison of student attitudes towards school, teachers, and peers in Swedish comprehensive schools now and 35 years ago. *Education Research, 48*(1), 55–75.

Klonsky, M. (2002). How small schools prevent violence. *Educational Leadership, 59*(5), 65–69.

Kristjansson, K. (2006, March). Emulations and the use of role models in education. *Journal of Moral Education, 35*(1), 37–49.

Lassen, S. R., Steele, M. M., & Sailor, W. (2006). The relationship between school-wide positive behavior support to academic achievement in an urban middle school. *Psychology in Schools, 43*(6), 701–712.

Laud, L. (1998, April). Changing the way we communicate. *Educational Leadership, 55*(7), 23–25.

Lebell, S. (1995). *The art of living: The classical manual on virtue, happiness, and effectiveness.* New York: HarperCollins.

Lickona, T. (1991). *Educating for character: How our schools can teach respect and responsibility.* New York: Bantam Books.

Lickona, T., & Davidson, M. (2005). *Smart and good high schools: Integrating excellence and ethics for success in schools, work, and beyond.* Cortland, NY: Center for 4th and 5th Rs (Respect and Responsibility).

Lickona, T., Schaps, E., and Lewis, C. (1994). *Eleven principals of effective character education.* Washington, DC: Character Education Partnership.

Lumsden, L. (1998, March). Teacher Morale. *ERIC Digest, 120,* p. 4.

Marzano, R. J. (2003). *Classroom management that works.* Alexandria, VA: Association for Supervision and Curriculum Development.

Maslow, A. H. (1943). A theory of human motivation. *Psychological Review, 50,* 370–396.

Murphy, J. M., Drake, J. E., & Weinkeke, K. M. (2005, July). *Academic and break-fast connection pilot: Final report on New York's classroom breakfast project.* Albany: Nutrition Consortium of New York State.

Myhrvold, A. N., Olsen, E., & Lauridsen, O. (1996). Indoor environment in schools: Pupil's health and performance in regard to CO_2 concentration. The seventh international conference on indoor air quality and climate. *Indoor Air, 4,* 369–371.

Nepo, D. (2007). *Facing the lion: Being the lion.* San Francisco: Conari Press.

No Child Left Behind Act. Section 5431. (2002). U.S. Department of Education.

Olweus, D. (1978). *Aggression in the schools: Bullying and whipping boys.* New York: John Wiley & Sons.

Ontario Ministry of Education Policy/Program Memorandum No. 144. (2007).

Palmer, P. J. (1998). *The courage to teach.* San Francisco: Jossey-Bass.

Palmer, P. J. (2000). *Let your life speak: Listening for the voice of vocation.* San Francisco: Jossey-Bass.

Reeves, D. (2006). *The learning leader: How to focus school improvement for better results.* Alexandria, VA. Association for Supervision and Curriculum Development.

Ruiz, D. (1997). *The four agreements.* San Rafael, CA: Allen Amber.

Ryan, K., & Bohlin, K. (2003). *Building character in schools.* New York: John Wiley & Sons.

Sagor, R. (2005). *The action research guidebook: A four-step process for educators and school teams.* Thousand Oaks, CA: Corwin.

Sample, S. B. (2001). *The contrarian's guide to leadership.* New York: John Wiley & Sons.

Senge, P. (1990). *The fifth discipline: The art and practice of the learning organization.* New York: Currency Doubleday.

Sharma, R. (2006). *The greatness guide.* Toronto, Ontario, Canada: HarperCollins.

Sharpiro, S., & Skinulis, K. (2000). *Classrooms that work: A teacher's guide to discipline without stress.* Richmond Hill, Ontario, Canada: Practical Parenting Program.

Short, P. M., & Greer, J. T. (1997). *Leadership in empowered schools: Themes for innovative efforts.* Upper Saddle River, NJ: Prentice Hall.

Stapley, L. (2006). *Individuals, groups, and organizations beneath the surface: An introduction.* London: The Studio Publishing Services.

Stormont, M., Lewis, T., Beckner, R., & Johnson, N. (2008). *Implementing positive behavior support systems in early childhood and elementary settings.* Thousand Oaks, CA; Corwin.

Sullivan, K. (2007, April). Character education: Models of imperfection. *School Arts: The Art Education Magazine for Teachers, 106*(8), 12.

Teacher Support Network. (2007). *British School Council for School Environments.* Retrieved December 2008, from www.teachersupports.info/files/upload/docs/0607_School_Environments_Reports.pdf.

The Faulkner report: The road to health: A final report on school safety. (2008). Toronto, Ontario, Canada: Toronto District School Board.

The heart of the matter: Character and citizenship education in Alberta schools. (2005). Edmonton, Alberta, Canada: Ministry of Education.

Tomlinson, C. A., & McTighe, J. (2006). *Integrating differentiated instruction: Understanding by design.* Alexandria, VA: Association for Supervision and Curriculum Development.

United States Department of Education. (2004). *A summary of scientific findings on adverse effects of indoor environments on students' health, academic performance and attendance.* United States Government.

Urban, H. (2003). *Life's greatest lessons.* New York: Simon & Schuster.

Vincent, P. (2003). *Rules and procedures for character education: The first step toward school civility.* (2nd ed.) Chapel Hill, NC: Character Development Group.

Vincent, P. F. (1999). *Developing character in students.* Chapel Hill, NC: Character Development Group.

Vincent, P. F. (2005). *Restoring school civility.* Chapel Hill, NC: Character Development Group.

Wargocki, P., Wyon, D. P., Matysiak, B., & Irgins, S. (2005). *The effects of classroom temperature and outdoor air supply rate on the performance of school work by children.* International Center for Indoor Environment and Energy, Technical University of Denmark: Anker Engelundsvej.

Welsh Office of Standards in Education. (2007, January). *An evaluation of performance of schools before and after moving into new buildings or significantly refurbished premises.* Her Majesty's Inspectorate for Education and Training in Wales. Cardiff, Wales: Estyn.

Whitaker, T. (2003). *What great principals do differently.* Larchmont, NY: Eye on Education.

Williams, R. D., & Taylor, R. T. (2003). *Leading with character to improve student achievement.* Chapel Hill, NC: Character Development Group.

Woolner, P., Hall, E., Higgins, S., & McCaughey, C. (2007, February). A solid foundation? What we know about the impact of environments on learning and the implications for building schools for the future. *Oxford Review of Education, 33*(1), 47–70.

Woolner, P., Hall, E., Wall, K., & Dennison, D. (2007). Getting together to improve the school environment: User consultation, participatory design and student voice. *Improving Schools, 10*(233), 223–248.

Young, E., Green, H. A., & Roderick-Patrick, L. (2003). *Tennessee Advisory Commission on Intergovernmental Relations.* (ED479494), p. 40.